THE DATA DELUGE

THE DATA DELUGE

Can Libraries Cope with E-Science?

Deanna B. Marcum and
Gerald George, Editors

Foreword by Kakugyo S. Chiku

LIBRARIES UNLIMITED
An Imprint of ABC-CLIO, LLC

A B C 〜 C L I O

Santa Barbara, California • Denver, Colorado • Oxford, England

Library of Congress Cataloging-in-Publication Data

The data deluge : can libraries cope with e-science? / Deanna B. Marcum and Gerald George, editors ;
  foreword by Kakugyo S. Chiku.
      p. cm.
  Includes bibliographical references and index.
  Papers delivered at the 2007 and 2008 International Roundtable on Library and Information Science
  at the Library Center of the Kanazawa Institute of Technology (KIT).
  ISBN 978–1–59158–887–0 (acid-free paper)
1. Science and technology libraries—Information technology—Congresses. 2. Communication in
science—Technological innovations—Congresses. 3. Information storage and retrieval systems—Science
—Congresses. 4. Science—Electronic information resources—Congresses. 5. Libraries and electronic
publishing—Congresses. 6. Cyberinfrastructure—Congresses. 7. Digital libraries—Congresses. 8.
Research libraries—United States—Case studies—Congresses. I. Marcum, Deanna B. II. George,
Gerald. III. Kanazawa Institute of Technology International Roundtable on Library and Information
Science.
Z675.T3D38   2010
026'.50285—dc22   2009040981

14 13 12 11 10   1 2 3 4 5

This book is also available on the World Wide Web as an eBook.
Visit www.abc-clio.com for details.

ABC-CLIO, LLC
130 Cremona Drive, P.O. Box 1911
Santa Barbara, California 93116-1911

This book is printed on acid-free paper ∞

Manufactured in the United States of America

CONTENTS

Foreword by Kakugyo S. Chiku   vii

Introduction   ix
   Deanna B. Marcum and Gerald George

PART I: OVERVIEW OF E-SCIENCE CHALLENGES FOR LIBRARIES   1

1   **Grand Challenges and New Roles for the Twenty-First-Century Research Library in an Era of E-Science**   3
   Richard E. Luce

2   **E-Science and Research Libraries: An Agenda for Action**   17
   Wendy Pradt Lougee

3   **The Challenges of E-Science Data Set Management and Scholarly Communication for Domain Sciences and Engineering: A Role for Academic Libraries and Librarians**   33
   James L. Mullins

4   **Changes in Research Libraries as a Result of E-Science Initiatives: A Snapshot**   43
   Neil Rambo

PART II: PERSPECTIVES FROM NATIONAL ORGANIZATIONS   61

5 Library and Information Technology Support of E-Science in the   63
   Western Context
   Joan K. Lippincott

6 Head in the Clouds and Boots on the Ground: Science,   77
   Cyberinfrastructure, and CLIR
   Amy Friedlander

PART III: PERSPECTIVES FROM INDIVIDUAL RESEARCH LIBRARIES   91

7 E-Science at Johns Hopkins University   93
   G. Sayeed Choudhury

8 An Idiosyncratic Perspective on the History and Development at   99
   University California, San Diego, of Support for Cyberinfrastructure-
   Enabled E-Science
   Brian E. C. Schottlaender

9 The National Agricultural Library and E-Science   113
   Peter R. Young

Index   131

About the Editors and Contributors   141

FOREWORD

Thanks to digital technology, information exchange has become increasingly global in increasingly large quantities. With this exciting development, however, have come challenges for research libraries whose traditional responsibility has been to acquire, organize, and preserve information for ongoing use. One of the challenges—a major one—comes from scientists employing the new technologies. How can librarians cope with vast databases generated by astronomers, oceanographers, and others participating in what we have come to call E-science? Do librarians even have a role in managing and making available such globally created and accessed information?

So important is this subject that for two years, 2007 and 2008, it has been the focus of the International Roundtable for Library and Information Science. Since 1994, the roundtable has been an annual event at the Library Center of the Kanazawa Institute of Technology (KIT) in Kanazawa, Japan; and since 2001, we have produced the roundtable in collaboration with the Council on Library and Information Resources (CLIR) in Washington, D.C. The roundtable has given Japanese librarians an opportunity to discuss common concerns with our counterparts in America and elsewhere who are invited to deliver papers.

This book contains the papers delivered in the two roundtables on E-science. This is the third volume of papers from the roundtable. We offer them to extend information and insight to others in the world who are also concerned with issues confronting digital-era libraries.* We hope to continue sponsoring

---

*The first two volumes were these: *Development of Digital Libraries: An American Perspective*, edited by Deanna B. Marcum (Westport, CT: Greenwood Press, 2001), and *Digital Library Development: The View from Kanazawa*, edited by Deanna B. Marcum and Gerald George (Westport, CT: Libraries Unlimited, 2006).

the roundtables annually in collaboration with our American colleagues and friends.

I am grateful to Deanna Marcum, now associate librarian of Congress for library services, who began CLIR's collaboration with us when she was CLIR's president. She has subsequently chaired committees to select the speakers, has joined us each year to introduce them, and has arranged for the papers' publication. I am grateful also to Charles Henry, the president of CLIR, for CLIR's continued support for the undertaking. I also want to express gratitude to my KIT colleagues in both the library and the university's administration for their contributions to the roundtables' success. And I particularly thank Mr. Koshiro Moroya, the assistant director of the KIT Library Center, who does so much to make the roundtables run so well.

Kakugyo S. Chiku
Director
Kanazawa Institute of Technology Library Center

INTRODUCTION

We used to think of scientists as standing in laboratories, observing chemical reactions in test tubes, and recording equations on blackboards, or traipsing through jungles and scribbling on notepads their observations of newly discovered species. Now another image is emerging—an image of scientists sitting before computers, clicking into huge digital databases of Internet-accessible information, and using electronic tools to make analyses never before possible, while conferring about problems and progress via Web networks with other scientists thousands of miles away.

The data they use—astonishing quantities of it measured in trillions of "bytes"—may come from telescopes that nightly sweep the sky, from weather recording devices in multiple locations, from efforts to track genetic variations among plants and animals, from devices that monitor changes in the earth's atmosphere, and from hundreds of other means by which scientists amass observations and information for electronic analysis. All this and related activities we now call *E-science*. The value of these networked data collections may extend far beyond the immediate scientific studies for which they were created. Many of them may remain valuable for centuries and for kinds of studies yet to be conceived.

Who will electronically acquire, evaluate, manage, and preserve all these sets of data for as long as they are needed? Who will maintain the "cyberinfrastructure" that makes the use possible? Who will provide ongoing points of access to so much data? Who will help scientists locate in such masses of material what they need and make collaborative as well as individual use of it? Do the world's research libraries have appropriate, even essential, roles in all this?

Such are the questions that necessitate this book.

Part I of the book provides four expert perspectives on the questions overall. First, Richard E. Luce, vice president and director of libraries at Emory University, introduces E-science in relation to libraries. Then Wendy Pradt Lougee, university librarian at the University of Minnesota—Twin Cities, expands on the challenges for libraries that E-science poses. Next, James L. Mullins, dean of libraries at Purdue University, looks closely at how libraries might aid E-scientists in particular fields. And Neil Rambo, acting director of health sciences libraries at the University of Washington, assesses whether libraries are adequately acting to meet E-science needs.

Part II of the book presents perspectives from national organizations concerned with E-science challenges to libraries. Joan K. Lippincott, associate executive director of the Coalition for Networked Information (CNI), describes her organization's concerns with the subject and reports on how organizations abroad are responding to E-science. Amy Friedlander, director of programs at the Council on Library and Information Resources (CLIR), describes E-science interests that CLIR is pursuing.

Part III of the book presents perspectives from individual research libraries that are attempting to deal supportively with E-science. G. Sayeed Choudhury, associate dean of University Libraries at Johns Hopkins University, describes E-science initiatives at his institution, their relation to its libraries, and the potential applicability of developments there to other institutions. Brian E. C. Schottlaender, university librarian at the University of California, San Diego, describes the evolution and current status of groundbreaking work there to develop cyberinfrastructure in support of E-science. And Peter R. Young, former director of the National Agricultural Library (NAL), describes strategies that NAL has developed to advance the role of research libraries in agricultural E-science.

All of these essays began as papers presented at the International Roundtable for Library and Information Science in 2007 and 2008 in Kanazawa, Japan. For many years now, the Kanazawa Institute of Technology (KIT) has annually hosted the roundtable, inviting speakers from the United States and elsewhere in the world, selected by a committee chaired by Deanna Marcum, associate librarian of Congress for library services. For more than a decade, the roundtable has focused on digital library development and associated aspects of the electronic-information era. All of us who have participated feel grateful to KIT, to Kakugyo S. Chiku, director of its Library Center, and to his associates for their professional perspicacity and their personal hospitality. Through this book we hope to make widely available the insights that emerged in the Kanazawa roundtables.

                                        Deanna B. Marcum and Gerald George, editors

PART I

OVERVIEW OF E-SCIENCE CHALLENGES FOR LIBRARIES

GRAND CHALLENGES AND NEW ROLES FOR THE TWENTY-FIRST-CENTURY RESEARCH LIBRARY IN AN ERA OF E-SCIENCE

Richard E. Luce

Abstract

The emergence of E-science is beginning to create a fourth branch of science, characterized by collaborative, data-driven networked research. E-science developments, enabled by the "next-generation" infrastructure, are generating massive amounts of data and require access to an aggregated set of distributed resources. The need to manage large data repositories and E-science work-flow services is an outgrowth of these developments, although it is unclear what organizational entities will emerge to take on these challenges.

For research libraries, these developments raise a number of profound challenges while providing an opportunity for libraries to redefine their roles and to provide an added dimension of value. Combining vision and strategic investments with a leveraging of their domain strengths in information management, digital libraries could become an essential resource among a set of many distributed, interoperable resources available to the next generation of research communities. This chapter outlines the factors driving this new reality and describes the resulting challenges that must be met to transform research libraries.

The Emergence of E-Science

For the past few centuries the methodological paradigms underpinning scientific inquiry could be characterized and divided into two realms: theoretical and experimental science. During the past two decades, computer simulation and mathematical modeling have evolved to support a third branch of science, known as computational science, which is characterized by efforts to model natural systems in the physical sciences and human systems in the social sciences, and to support the development of new technologies in process engineering.

Today recognition is increasing that a fourth branch of science, E-science, has begun to emerge. Characterized by global collaboration, it is supported by the next generation of infrastructure (computational, storage, and data transfer capacity, coupled with information tools, instruments, and sensors), which enables collaborative, networked science. The term *E-science* is attributable to John Taylor, who used it to describe a United Kingdom funding initiative in 2000. E-science is characterized as computationally intense science employing grid computing technology to analyze very large data collections.[1] It can be further characterized by large-scale, distributed collaboration via the Internet combined with key supporting technologies, such as high-performance computing and large-scale information management. In the United States, *cyberinfrastructure* is the term used to denote this infrastructure. The infrastructure is intended to empower scientists to do their research faster, better, and in different ways.

The practice of science involves the articulation of a problem (based on scientific theory and literature), instrumentation, measurement, data management, analysis, and knowledge dissemination. As these functions are increasingly conducted using computing technology, the computationally based laboratory is becoming the norm. Moving these capabilities and work flow to the Internet creates the virtual laboratory, and distributed virtual laboratories represent another manifestation of E-science. Current developments supporting E-science include the use of digital laboratory notebooks, which capture information at its source, while providing direct access to raw data sets through links and metadata.

Data Generation and E-Science

At the CERN laboratory in Geneva, the world's most powerful particle accelerator—the Large Hadron Collider (LHC)—has been constructed. High-energy physics experiments at the LHC will be on a scale greater than any previous physics experiments, and each experiment will generate several petabytes of data per year. The major experiments are collaborations involving more than 1,000 physicists from more than 100 institutions in Europe, America, and Asia. The experimental data initially generated at CERN will be distributed to groups of scientists all over the world.

Moving along a similar vector, biomedicine has experienced explosive growth, supported in large part by an increase in capabilities associated with bioinformatics. Bioinformatics seeks to enable the discovery of new biological insights by merging the fields of computational biology, computer science, and information science and technology to form a single discipline. Biology in the twenty-first century is experiencing a transformation from a purely lab-based science to an information science, and the field has developed an unprecedented capacity to characterize biologic systems at their most fundamental levels with the use of tools and technologies almost unimaginable a generation ago. These developments are already having a profound effect on formal communication and publishing. Increasingly, biomedical journals require primary data to be deposited on the publisher's or investigator's Web-accessible site.[2]

Other examples abound in new fields such as earth systems and climate modeling, biogeochemistry, and computational pathomics—which have further increased the requirements that are demanded of associated databases and data repositories. A report from the National Science Board declares:

> It is exceedingly rare that fundamentally new approaches to research and education arise. Information technology has ushered in such a fundamental change. Digital data collections are at the heart of this change. They enable analysis at unprecedented levels of accuracy and sophistication and provide novel insights through innovative information integration. Through their very size and complexity, such digital collections provide new phenomena for study.[3]

The rise of very large sets of data, which grow in size and complexity at an extraordinary rate, is a distinguishing characteristic in the development of E-science. This development is leading toward an inevitable data deluge. For example, in biology, hundreds of gigabytes of genome-sequence data are available online via the Web; in astronomy, hundreds of terabytes of digital observatory data are available through sites such as the U.S. National Virtual Observatory.[4] The goal of the Large Synoptic Survey Telescope project is to map the visible sky every three nights.[5] By the year 2010, 20–30 terabytes of images will be captured each night.[6] The availability of these vast data sets via the Internet, coupled with new computationally derived data-mining tools, is transforming many areas of science by providing insights at a level of detail inconceivable only a decade earlier.

Managing the Data Deluge

Our data-dominant era presents new challenges for scientists, the research community, data custodians, and digital data repositories. A report in *Science* magazine declared:

> In order to exploit and explore the petabytes of scientific data that will arise from these high-throughput experiments, supercomputer simulations, sensor networks, and satellite surveys, scientists will need assistance from specialized search engines, data mining tools, and data visualization tools that make it easy to ask questions and understand answers.[7]

During the early phase of these developments, research scientists generally managed experimental data manually, seeking to identify potentially interesting features and discover significant relationships between them. However, with the increases in scale and complexity generated through simulations and a constant data flow emanating from always-on sensors, manual methods are proving to be inadequate.

As the automated mechanisms for capturing and analyzing streaming data are developed, issues surrounding standardized labeling and identifying contents correspondingly grow in scale and complexity. Automatically annotated scientific data that describe interesting features are required, and these annotations need to be augmented with enriched metadata containing descriptive comments that give context to the resulting information. Finally, new tools will need to be developed that enable scientists to progress beyond the generation of structured information toward the automated knowledge management of scientific data. In the words of a study by T. Hey and A. E. Trefethen, "One of the key drivers behind the search for such new scientific tools is the imminent deluge of data from new generations of scientific experiments and surveys."[8]

In order to create tools that effectively search, categorize, and give context to this data, highly enriched annotated metadata are required to describe provenance, contents, formats, usage conditions, rights, and so forth. Specifying these requirements up front, as well as creating taxonomies to support cross-disciplinary research, requires the skills and knowledge of information scientists in the broadest sense. Those skills include the ability to merge aspects of many disciplines, including library science, computer science, informatics, and cognitive and social sciences.

It is a given that the research communities will need to store and to access these data sets in repositories somewhere, analogous to today's storing of journal articles and citations by digital libraries. The ability to access, manipulate, and mine this data is a central requirement for the new generation of collaborative, networked science applications. It is also a given that scientists generally and strongly desire to focus on their science work and would prefer to leave the details of data management, curation, and long-term infrastructure maintenance problems to others.

Starting with Guiding Principles

With a great number of possible options and scenarios confronting the strategic choices that need to be made, a few guiding principles ought to shape our thinking and direction.

Principle One: Leadership and vision will be required to formulate a long-term strategic framework for scientific data management and the corresponding development of a strategic roadmap for the implementation and evolution of data repositories. The evolution of data repositories will need to confront the issues of centralized or federated distributed repositories, as well as what organizations will be most appropriate as partners. To be successful, localized data repository developments must be user-centric and driven by the research needs of the communities they have been organized to support.

Principle Two: The principle that data is a public good goes hand-in-hand with the view that the E-science infrastructure is a shared common good. The principle of equitable open access to publicly funded scientific data should be adopted wherever possible. This principle should be taken into consideration in the development of data repositories and ancillary services and systems.

Principle Three: Standards and standards-based technologies will need to be adopted and their use should be widely promoted to ensure interoperability between data and metadata management systems. At the same time we need to ensure that these systems support authentication and data protection, with safeguards reliably built in and periodically validated. For these purposes, libraries' successful history of identifying and brokering standards and establishing collaborative relationships should position them well.

New Roles for Research Libraries

Many challenges, driven by the relentless evolution of information and computing technologies, profoundly impact the role of the research library today. Among the more obvious challenges is Google's book-digitization program, which, when coupled with Google's ubiquitous presence and organization of information in the broader context, presents an alternative to the role of libraries in information delivery. The grand challenge of providing data services in the era of E-science is stretching the question of the research library's role even further.

Computational techniques and resources, the generation and use of massive data sets, increasing reliance on interdisciplinary teams, and interinstitutional and international collaborations—all these things added together are transforming the way science is practiced. As these new forms of science speed up the discovery and communication processes, they add to the complexity of the challenge. Libraries will not be immune from change in this new world of data-enabled research; on the contrary, the scale of change confronting research libraries is unprecedented.

New Organizational Structures

It is likely that new hybrid organizations will emerge to tackle the questions surrounding long-term custodianship of data repositories, although it is premature to predict which organization(s) will succeed at the task. Any number of organizations could combine the capabilities needed to ensure success, including commercial ventures, supercomputer centers, research libraries, dedicated research groups, or new organizations.

At this stage, libraries should focus on developing the functional requirements of a data-archiving infrastructure and let the appropriate organizational forms emerge from those requirements. As with any new paradigm shift, there are many opportunities and challenges for both new players and for those organizations that have the agility to adapt and move quickly. The organizational model that research libraries have operated under—managing collections based on a disciplinary focus—doesn't fit the needs of scientists in this new paradigm and is not in line with the transformation that is occurring in the sciences.

Changes in scientific-research libraries, as they evolve from digital versions of traditional services, must be driven by and reflect the more fundamental changes in the conduct of science and the associated needs of the research communities they enable. Scientists will expect the same ubiquitous convenience and advanced capabilities from their reconstructed digital library as they are able to obtain from widely available E-science work flows.

Collaboration, cooperation, and standards are needed to exploit heterogeneous sources of data, but the difficulties of cooperation are often ignored and the benefits often fall short of expectations. Many types of organizations have expertise in some dimension of data-driven scholarship: research centers, libraries, supercomputing centers, archives, Internet companies, etc. But in almost every instance such expertise is incidental to the major expertise of the organization. The challenges facing research libraries in supporting science are to articulate and to advance their role in the virtual laboratory environment. Success will require developing a deep anticipatory understanding of what researchers need in their virtual laboratory.

Changing Landscape for Scholarly Communication

The nature of scholarly publishing and communication continues to evolve dramatically. Not only is publication on the Web, in various forms, enabling access to a much wider range of research literature, but also we are seeing the emergence of data archives as a complementary form of scholarly communication.

The Berlin Declaration on Open Access to Knowledge in the Sciences and Humanities was drafted in 2003 "to promote the Internet as a functional instrument for a global scientific knowledge base and human reflection and to specify measures which research policy makers, research institutions, funding agencies, libraries, archives and museums need to consider." As of May 2007, 230 organizations from all over the world had signed the Berlin Declaration. It is noteworthy that the Berlin Declaration is not just concerned with text publications. The declaration defines open access contributions to include "original scientific research results, raw data and metadata, source materials, digital representations of pictorial and graphical materials and scholarly multimedia material." Such bodies of material will contain hundreds or thousands of terabytes of data, which will need to be archived.[9]

There is a shift in importance from the publication(s) of a research project to the data-modeling and data-generation phases that occur earlier in the research life cycle. This shift to a more dynamic and collaborative process of doing science has led to a loose and more informal means of communicating. In some areas of science this is leading to a less well-defined medium that is part publication and part an ongoing communication process. Supporting this shift requires supporting these communication processes in a more active way, as opposed to just archiving the end result of this work in a formal publication. Librarians and informaticians need to be involved in the early planning and data-modeling phases of the work in order to play a more vital integration role.

Opportunities

Data used to be hidden behind the office or laboratory walls, in notebooks and file cabinets, and on hard drives. Now the data are more often "loose" and may be available to be repurposed and recombined. An immediate and important challenge associated with caring for data is how to provide end-to-end scientific data management, from data acquisition and data integration to data treatment, provenance, persistence, and digital preservation. How might libraries respond to this challenge?

In many research fields there are national repositories responsible for the curation and preservation of those fields' scientific materials, as well as domain repositories. University libraries, on the other hand, may need to take responsibility for assisting with the curation and preservation of smaller-scale data repositories arising from the work of local research groups. The scientific library intending to remain relevant must play a significant role in building capacity of that kind. The desired linkages between research outputs and associated data require the assignment of compatible descriptive and terminological elements. A high level of description used with research data is critical for enabling users to discover new ways of combining and using data. Libraries are well positioned to initiate this strategic work.

Access to a distributed collection of data is highly dependent upon uniform methods of description. This is equally true for the preservation of the data. Metadata are an essential component of research data. The library can take an important lead in the development of standardized, automated metadata for the virtual observatory. Developing and managing metadata are established tasks in the library community, although a far greater emphasis on machine-aided creation and maintenance will be required to handle metadata on the scale envisioned.

High on the priority list ought to be the formulation of new partnerships with researchers—in all fields—who are data-driven. We can learn much about their needs, by watching how they work as well as by talking with them. In addition to building and maintaining institutional data repositories, libraries can enable collaborative networks and provide communication space (both virtual and physical) in which researchers can work.

The people responsible for managing such data repository collections are beginning to be called data scientists. They could just as well be data librarians or informaticians.

Whatever label is used, this is an emerging profession without many members, and the library could play a significant role in building data-management capacity. The data collections in virtual laboratories tend to be distributed, which requires a coordinating role across institutions. Libraries have a long tradition of creatively coordinating resource sharing across multiple institutions and they could play a similar role in the realm of distributed data collections.

Research libraries might actively provide project support, although they are not typically organized to do this. An example is the need for librarians to join virtual research teams that form dynamically to support the initial planning phases of a research project, work on a project (e.g., with a research team that is gearing up), and then change into something else when a less intense presence is needed. This requires a fluid staffing structure and a more dynamic model for academic libraries than their current practice of maintaining departmental subject liaisons. Subject librarians may be well integrated with academic departments but are not typically able to respond dynamically to emerging kinds of research with intense needs.

Today many research libraries are struggling with the challenges of trying to respond to the work-flow needs of E-scientists. Given scarcity of human resources, attempting to respond within the framework of a single institution may be too limiting. The question arises, how can we connect institutions with similar needs and pool the development of tools and resources within a shared environment? In the following paragraphs I will describe a few challenges to consider.

Repositories, Work Flow, and Data Archiving

Libraries have traditionally been a source for storing and providing access to archived publications. More recently, libraries have played a role in supporting pre-published materials. An example is the Physics Preprint Archive, part of the arXiv located at Cornell.[10] The scale and complexity of E-science data repositories will require new, professionally hybrid teams to cope with organizing and curating these assets. Successful efforts will become multi-institutional and international in scope, weaving together complex relationships of organizations and repositories that mirror today's highly networked Web world. New financial models will be required to enable repositories to keep pace with double-digit growth in storage and computing infrastructures.

Among the services offered by today's libraries, several capabilities necessary to support E-science are missing. For example, how can researchers effectively locate profiles of scientists and other groups working on common problems outside one's field of expertise? Where can one locate a comprehensive registry description of deployed sensors or a registry of data sets with a description of use conditions? Analyses of data and data visualizations are available on the Web, but are scattered and uncoordinated.

The next generation of digital libraries, supporting data repositories, needs to be integrated within the grid architecture to enable collaborative work flows. E-science libraries will provide a combination of user applications and digital object repositories with both human and machine interfaces. Information will flow into and out of these digital library repositories, enabled by machine interfaces as well as by social software that supports humans working collaboratively.

Finding Relevant Sources

Even in the Google era it is difficult to identify suitable data sources and well-described repositories via the Web. A first step in building models that support transdisciplinary science requires the researcher to locate relevant data repositories and databases outside of one's own field. One critical component of the emerging cyberinfrastructure is the array of instruments and sensors deployed on the grid. We need to create a global registry of instruments and sensors so that scientists and scientists-in-training can obtain information about them, including how to use them. At a minimum, a description of the relevant data set or database contents and the way in which the data are produced and/or derived from other data sources is mandatory.

Unfortunately, well-described global registries are not the norm and not every database provides such meta-information.

Since science has increasingly become interdisciplinary, communication challenges arise in terms of linguistic labels as well as conceptually. Semantics and the need for taxonomies continue to grow in importance.

Self-Correcting Databases

In the words of the 2020 Science Group, "A revolution is taking place in the scientific method. 'Hypothesize, design and run experiment, analyze results' is being replaced by 'hypothesize, look up answer in database.'"[11]

It seems obvious that we need close bidirectional communication between database providers and users to address problems and correct errors. While the Web 2.0 world has begun to adopt social software and connectedness as a means of collaborating, many providers in the database world still desire to control their silos and consequently are not open about their data-curation processes, nor about schema and content changes. Error reporting and tracking need to be a fundamental prerequisite for continuity.

Curation Requires Funding

The importance of databases is fundamental to entire disciplines such as chemistry and biology. However, long-term curation efforts are rarely supported, and most publicly available database providers have funding problems. Funding for long-term curation of data repositories and scientific databases is required, and one can only wonder what the eventual state of massively scaled data repositories (and the integrity of the science they support) will be a decade hence if this is ignored. An equally perplexing issue is the curatorial question of what is to be kept and what is to be tossed.

Education and Training

The rise of data science coupled with the challenges above will require libraries and educators to address the need for informaticians and informationists. Many problems that users experience with scientific databases can be traced to a lack of interest in and basic understanding of data management on the part of scientific experts involved, while participating informaticians may not be aware of the domain needs. Because communication difficulties that arise from these problems clearly have educational roots, the learning curricula for both informaticians and research scientists should be better defined to equip future practitioners.

Digital Library Augmentation through Collaboration Support

The new generation of digital library services must support evolving E-science communities. Leading-edge examples of new E-science digital library activities that support virtual laboratories can be found at the Sheridan Libraries in the Johns Hopkins University and at the Los Alamos National Laboratory Research Library. As I and my colleagues have written in the *International Journal of Digital Libraries*:

> Digital libraries are one of the many distributed, interoperable eScience resources that facilitate both human and machine collaboration . . . In terms of human collaboration, collaborative workspaces provide a social component to digital libraries that expands their role in a manner consistent with the collaborative nature of eScience by facilitating collaborative discussion, discovery, and collection development.[12]

Providing collaborative support for geographically distributed colleagues, in a working environment that is augmented by social software, is one of the key capabilities required by scientists. Project-oriented collaborative work spaces are useful in meeting this need. To provide a social component to digital library services, two kinds of collaborative work spaces and resources were experimentally prototyped at Los Alamos: work spaces facilitating collaborative content discovery, and work spaces facilitating collaborative content creation.[13]

The most commonly used social software tools on the Web have been designed to support social behavior; for example, this is applied to the practice of science to help scientists, regardless of their fields, write grant proposals, analyze data, and coauthor papers. What is needed are developments that support a spectrum of activities with one end characterized by the use of automation and the virtual organization of services, and the other end characterized by interaction among virtual organizations of people. To quote the report of a 2007 conference on human-computer interaction:

> Since collaborative workspaces created for specific purposes are used more frequently than those created for general discussion, it is important to include support for the kinds of tasks that scientists frequently perform, such as annotating datasets. The Karst Collaborative Workspace, a collaborative endeavor with scientists and librarians at the University of New Mexico, is being designed to allow users to annotate image datasets and to archive their annotations with their datasets.[14]

An Evolutionary Direction—the Adaptive Web

While we are in the early stages of developing the new paradigm(s) required to support data science, and constructing solutions for massively scaled data repositories, we have the opportunity (and obligation) to creatively reconceptualize our approach, lest we magnify the current limitations in the scholarly communication chain. Increasingly, value resides in the relationships between researchers, experimental data, papers, and the ancillary supporting materials, as well as in the associated dialogue from comments, reviews, and updates to the original work.[15] Typically, when hypertext browsing is used to follow links manually for subject headings, thesauri, and textual concepts and categories, the user can traverse only a small portion of a large knowledge space. To manage and utilize the potentially rich and complex nodes and connections in a large knowledge system such as the distributed Web, system-aided reasoning methods would be useful to suggest relevant knowledge intelligently to the user.

As our systems grow more sophisticated, we will see applications that support not just links between authors and papers but applications supporting dynamic relationships between users and repositories of data and information, and between users and communities. What is required is a mechanism to enable active communication between these relationships and the aggregated knowledge these relationships contain that leads to information exchange, adaptation, and recombination—which, in itself, will constitute a new type of data repository of relationships. New generations of information retrieval tools and applications are being designed that will support self-organizing knowledge on distributed networks driven by human interaction.[16] This capability would allow a physicist or biochemist to collaborate with colleagues in the life sciences without having to learn an entirely new vocabulary.

Recent notable examples of the success of decentralized efforts with innovative approaches include such diverse experiences as decoding the human genome, developing the open-source movement, and establishing peer-to-peer networks. It is in our long-term interest to optimize the ability of our communication systems to support a variety of approaches while we develop our understanding of the coming adaptive Web and its impact on building data repositories that support both current and new forms of scientific communication. If we believe it is prudent to hedge our bets, many alternatives should be propagated and stimulated.

Conclusion

The emergence of E-science with associated large data repositories heralds not only a new way of doing science but also a challenging and exciting new world for libraries—provided that they seize these opportunities. Traditional roles played by the library—organizing information, providing access, and ensuring preservation—must be augmented by new capabilities for automatically describing, annotating, and manipulating a wide spectrum of collaborative, data-intensive information resources and relationships. The ability to discover and track research results across the gamut of resources from raw data to informal and formal communications remains an essential, although radically different looking, component of the research infrastructure. A powerful user-centric infrastructure that supports collaborative multidisciplinary science is now required. A grand challenge now faces us: the E-science revolution will put data repositories on center stage in the development of the next-generation research infrastructure.

Notes

NB: Internet addresses in the following notes and references were accurate as of December 10, 2008.

1. Summary based on the definition provided by the UK National e-Science Centre on its Web site: http://www.nesc.ac.uk/nesc/define.html.

2. Kenneth H. Buetow, "Cyberinfrastructure: Empowering a 'Third Way' in Biomedical Research," *Science* 308 (May 6, 2005): 821–24.

3. National Science Board, *Long-Lived Digital Data Collections: Enabling Research and Education in the 21st Century* (NSB-05-40), National Science Foundation, September 2005, http://www.nsf.gov/pubs/2005/nsb0540/start.jsp.

4. U.S. National Virtual Observatory Web site: http://www.us-vo.org/.

5. Large Synoptic Survey Telescope Web site: http://www.lsst.org/.

6. Alex Szalay, "Science in an Exponential World," presentation at the Seventh Annual AISTI Mini-Conference, Santa Fe, New Mexico, April 13, 2006. The LSST project is described at http://www.lsst.org/lsst/science/concept_data.

7. Tony Hey and Anne E. Trefethen, "Cyberinfrastructure for eScience," *Science* 308 (May 6, 2005): 817–21.

8. Tony Hey and Anne. E. Trefethen, "The Data Deluge," in *Grid Computing: Making the Global Infrastructure a Reality,* ed. F. Berman, G. Fox, and T. Hey (Hoboken, NJ: John Wiley, 2003), 809–824.

9. The quotations are from the "Berlin Declaration on Open Access to Knowledge in the Sciences and Humanities," October 20–22, 2003, http://www.zim.mpg.de/openaccess-berlin/berlindeclaration.html.

10. Available at http://xxx.lanl.gov. Also see Richard E. Luce, "Preprint Servers and Extensions to Other Fields," in *Electronic Scientific, Technical, and Medical Journal Publishing and Its Implications: Report of a Symposium* (Committee on Electronic Scientific, Technical, and Medical Journal Publishing: National Academies Press, April 2004), 70–72, http://www.nap.edu/openbook.php?record_id=10983&page=105.

11. The 2020 Science Group, *Towards Science 2020*, Microsoft Corporation (2006), 15, http://research.microsoft.com/towards2020science/downloads/T2020S_Report.pdf.

12. Linn Marks Collins et al., "Collaborative eScience Libraries," *International Journal on Digital Libraries* 7, no. 1 (2007), doi: 10.1007/s00799-007-0020-y, http://www.springerlink.com/content/2670604740777435/. URL points to SpringerLink (requires license for access).

13. Ibid.

14. Linn Marks Collins, "The Karst Collaborative Workspace for Analyzing and Annotating Scientific Datasets," lecture notes in computer science 4558 (2007): doi: 10.1007/978-3-540-73354-6. (Can be found through SpringerLink Series; requires authorized access.)

15. Richard E. Luce, "Evolution and Scientific Literature: Towards a Decentralized Adaptive Web" (in a series of articles called "Future E-access to the Primary Literature"), *Nature* (May 10, 2001), http://www.nature.com/nature/debates/e-access/Articles/luce.html.

16. Ibid.

Additional Reading

Atkins, Daniel E., Kelvin K. Droegemeier, Stuart I. Feldman, Hector Garcia-Molina, Michael L. Klein, David G. Messerschmitt, Paul Messina, Jeremiah P. Ostriker, and Margaret H. Wright, *Revolutionizing Science and Engineering through Cyberinfrastructure: Report of the National Science Foundation Blue Ribbon Advisory Panel on Cyberinfrastructure.* January 2003. www.nsf.gov/cise/sci/reports/atkins.pdf.

Foster, Ian. "Service-Oriented Science." *Science* 308, no. 5723 (May 6, 2005): 814–17.

Hey, Tony, and Anne Trefethen. "The Data Deluge." In *Grid Computing: Making the Global Infrastructure a Reality*, edited by Fran Berman, Geoffrey Fox, and Tony Hey, 809–24. Hoboken, NJ: John Wiley, 2003.

Luce, Richard, and M. Di Giacomo. "Personalized and Collaborative Digital Library Capabilities: Responding to the Changing Nature of Scientific Research." Special issue, *Issues in Science and Technology Libraries* 24, no. 1/2 (2003): doi: 10.1300/J122v24n01_09.

NSF Cyberinfrasture Council. *NSF's Cyberinfrastructure Vision for 21st Century Discovery.* National Science Foundation. Version 7.1, July 20, 2006. http://www.nsf.gov/od/oci/ci-v7.pdf.

President's Information Technology Advisory Committee. *Report to the President. Computational Science: Ensuring America's Competitiveness.* June 2005. http://www.nitrd.gov/pitac/reports/20050609_computational/computational.pdf.

Rocha, Luis M., and John Bollen. "Biologically Motivated Distributed Designs for Adaptive Knowledge Management." In *Design Principles for the Immune System and Other Distributed Autonomous Systems*, edited by Irun Cohen and L. A. Segel. New York: Oxford University Press, 2001.

Szalay, Alexander, and Jim Gray. "The World Wide Telescope." *Science* 293 (September 14, 2001): 2037–40.

CHAPTER 2

E-SCIENCE AND RESEARCH LIBRARIES: AN AGENDA FOR ACTION

Wendy Pradt Lougee

The emergence of E-science reflects a new era of science. Born from the convergence of multiple forces—notably advances in computational and communication technologies —E-science tests existing structures and models within the scientific community. E-science also challenges the research library community and its traditional modes of support. This chapter will focus on that complex relationship between emergent trends in E-science and the corresponding modifications prompted within the research library community.

Tony and Jessie Hey (Hey and Hey 2006) have described E-science as a new, fourth research methodology, one which is driven by networked capabilities and vast amounts of data. They note that well-established experimental and theoretical methodologies have been stretched in recent decades by computational methods, and now an era of large-scale, data-driven, and computationally intense science is taking shape. E-science fundamentally alters the ways in which scientists interact, the tools they employ, the types of problems they address, and the nature of the documentation and publication that result from their research. E-science requires new strategies for research support and significant development of infrastructure.

Nearly all aspects of the research library's classic functions and roles are influenced by these new methodologies. E-science embraces a multidisciplinary approach with significant reliance on computational science. Libraries have traditionally been structured and staffed around disciplines, and their computational involvements are modest by comparison. E-science is data-intensive, yet libraries have generally not collected nor been responsible for the management and preservation of scientific data. E-science is often conducted in a team context, with members of the team distributed across multiple institutions around the world. For libraries, the primary user constituency is typically comprised of those affiliated with the local institution. Further, the boundaries of licenses for electronic content, and the corresponding infrastructure for authentication and authorization, have usually been developed to meet the needs of individual institutions and do not currently translate well to a multi-institutional environment.

My plan in this overview is to explore the landscape of E-science and associated requirements for cyberinfrastructure in the context of the issues raised for research libraries. Lessons learned from library engagement in digital library development will be analyzed as a potentially similar process to understand how the E-science challenges might be addressed and what phases of library involvement can be anticipated. The work of the E-Science Task Force of the Association of Research Libraries (ARL) will be outlined to provide an early description of the agenda for engagement and action within the North American research library community.

General Landscape Trends

During the last few decades, several critical trends have laid the groundwork for E-science and its associated infrastructure. While such trends are well-reported in the literature, it is worth highlighting several major themes that are prominent within the academy and that, in particular, have had a concurrent impact on research library roles.

Distributed computing technologies provided a catalyst for change in the way information was created, managed, and shared. No longer dependent on local systems, the widespread access to computer-power and the development of network technologies "democratized" the Internet. With the birth of the World Wide Web, a new era of information access and delivery took shape. Emergent document standards, access protocols, and archiving techniques—to name several key developments— helped create an online environment that bridged differences between systems. These developments set the stage for distributed management and dissemination of information resources.

A second major shift occurred with the emergence of "open" paradigms. By this I mean models that make resources freely accessible and often involve collaborative exchange. For example, open-source software is collaboratively developed and freely shared. The Open Archives Initiative originated in response to the limitations of the traditional, commercial journal industry, with the intent to prompt nonrestrictive methods for distribution and use of research publications. Protocols emerged for sharing and retrieving information as well as a new genre for publishing: so-called eprints. These open paradigms set the stage for collaboration as a methodology for scholarly activity and research.

As control of and access to information became more distributed, and open models of exchange became more common, another critical trend emerged. There is in these open trends evidence of a shift from an emphasis on publication as *product* to publication as *process*. Computer scientist Hal Berghel (2001) has forecast that this shift will become increasingly prominent:

> By 2100, our current view of electronic publications as copyright-able artifacts will be viewed primarily as a historical allegiance to a pre-participatory, non-interactive,

essentially dull and lifeless era of publishing—an era in which one thought of digital libraries . . . as a collection of linked "things" rather than articulated processes and procedures. The current digital publication will be a relic, an obscure by-product from the horse and buggy age of digital networks. (p. 18)

There is evidence that this notion of "articulated processes and procedures" is already taking shape. We have countless examples of new genres of publishing that are interactive and can involve contributions and commentary from a distributed community of users. These publications may also have other associated components such as data or tools to interact with the data.

Another more recent trend, so-called social computing (sometimes referenced as "Web 2.0"), is fueling the open and process-oriented dimensions of the online environment. Social features are often embedded in networked systems and services, creating the capacity for group work and offering early functionality for virtual communities. We see in these contexts the possibilities for members of a group to interact with each other and with relevant information. Social tools also allow members of a group to develop and sustain a shared online environment through collective activity.

The above trends have enabled the library to be far more engaged in the *processes* of research rather than to have a singular focus on the *products* of research. We see significant investment of libraries in managing access to distributed content, in supporting open access to published research, and in the development of services to support the research process. For example, services such as the development of discipline-based repositories may provide an important foundation for future support of E-science virtual communities.

These general trends provide useful background as we review the major forces at play in the development of E-science because the trends have shaped the individual behaviors of scientists as well as the practices within disciplines.

The Landscape of E-Science and Cyberinfrastructure

It is important to understand the trends and characteristics of E-science that are particularly relevant to potential library roles. John Taylor, director general of research councils in the United Kingdom's Office of Science and Technology, is credited with coining the term *E-science*. In his own words, "e-science is about global collaboration in key areas of science and the next generation of infrastructure that will enable it" (Taylor 2005). Taylor and others have also suggested that E-science offers the potential to truly transform science.

In the United States, the National Science Foundation (NSF) has played a lead role in articulating the imperative for investment in E-science and its associated infrastructure, called *cyberinfrastructure*. The seminal report, *Revolutionizing Science and Engineering through Cyberinfrastructure*, was the result of an NSF Blue Ribbon Advisory Panel on Cyberinfrastructure (National Science Foundation 2003). This report set the stage in documenting the components of cyberinfrastructure that will need attention. It proposed to "use cyberinfrastructure to build more ubiquitous, comprehensive digital environments that become interactive and functionally complete for research communities in terms of people, data, information, tools, and instruments that operate at unprecedented levels of computational, storage, and data transfer capacity." Further, the report noted that emerging E-science projects "require effective federation of both distributed resources (data and facilities) and distributed, multidisciplinary expertise, and that cyberinfrastructure is a key to making this possible" (National Science Foundation 2003, p. ES3). Libraries have potential roles to play in both arenas cited—that is, in the development of both the technology and organizational infrastructure.

A more recent NSF report, *Cyberinfrastructure Vision for 21st Century Discovery*, lays out a more detailed plan of action (National Science Foundation 2007). Four interdependent areas of investment are specified:

- *high-performance computing*: investments here will focus on petascale capabilities for science and engineering
- *data, data analysis, and visualization*: investments here will cover work on data/metadata/ ontologies, data collections, and the development of a national digital data framework
- *virtual organizations for distributed communities*: investments here will focus on tools and technology systems for collaboration as well as evaluative research on the social and organizational dimensions of virtual communities
- *learning and workforce development*: investments here will prepare professionals who will support, deploy, develop, and design cyberinfrastructure. Further, investments will foster educational applications of cyberinfrastructure to enable the next generation of E-scientists

In addition to setting priorities for investment, the federal government also plays a role through policy. Policy can, for example, create both regulations and incentives for sharing data and making research results more freely accessible. NSF's current position on data indicates that:

> all science and engineering data generated with NSF funding must be made broadly accessible and usable, while being suitably protected and preserved. Through a suite of coherent policies designed to recognize different data needs and requirements within communities, NSF will promote open access to well-managed data . . . In addition to addressing the technological challenges inherent in the creation of a national data framework, NSF's data policies will be designed as necessary to mitigate existing sociological and cultural barriers to data sharing and access. (National Science Foundation 2007)

Trends in E-science are also shaped by sociological forces and normative behaviors within scientific disciplines. Such norms can inhibit the sharing of data and can also affect how effectively multidisciplinary teams that are geographically distributed can work together. For example, a recent assessment of the LEAD project (Linked Environments for Atmospheric Discovery) illustrates the organizational and social dimensions of scientific collaboration (Lawrence, Finholt, and Kim 2007). Difficulties cited included the lack of a central authority for coordinating "team science," challenges in effectively using communication technologies, and problems in coordinating work across institutions. To the extent to which libraries may play a future role in these virtual communities, it is important to anticipate where obstacles are likely to arise.

One final comment about the development of cyberinfrastructure may be instructive: there are undoubtedly lessons to be learned in studying other infrastructure developments in history. A recent workshop (Edwards et al. 2007) explored this question and highlighted the typical phases that technology infrastructure development entails. An initial phase is characterized by the formation of systems and the design of technology-based services. That phase is often followed by technology transfer across domains and the emergence of competing systems. A third phase sees consolidation of systems and the establishment of gateways that allow dissimilar systems to be linked into networks. In this latter phase, standardization and interorganizational communication are critical. The goal should be a mature infrastructure that is ubiquitous, accessible, reliable, and transparent. Importantly, NSF has anticipated this evolutionary path, and the likely obstacles that scientific disciplines will experience, in establishing its funding priorities. NSF expects to fund evaluative research on the social and organizational dimensions of virtual communities.

Developing Digital Library Infrastructure and Programs

The recent development of digital libraries may provide an informative case study. Digital library requirements for infrastructure and expertise created a challenge for research libraries that may have similarities to the challenges of E-science. Notably, many of the components of digital libraries also are prerequisites for E-science development.

Although there are early antecedents of digital libraries dating well back into the mid-twentieth century, it was largely the last three decades that have seen substantial progress. Clifford Lynch (Lynch 2005) notes that early work in library automation, online catalogs, and standards laid necessary groundwork, as did early investments in digitization and information retrieval systems. The World Wide Web provided a common platform through which to provide access to distributed information systems originating from universities as well as from the private sector (such as commercial publishers). The Web quickly captured the attention of a broader public beyond higher education.

NSF's programmatic funding (in collaboration with the Defense Advanced Research Projects Agency, the National Aeronautics and Space Administration, the National Library of Medicine, the National Institutes of Health, the Library of Congress, the National Endowment for the Humanities, and the Institute of Museum and Library Services) brought competitive support to digital library research and applications. As Lynch notes, the majority of NSF funding went to computer science groups, with libraries often being only peripherally involved. Nevertheless, substantial work proceeded in developing systems, document standards, metadata schema, identifiers, and other essentials for bringing standardization and interoperability to the digital library arena.

Using the classic phases of infrastructure development noted above, we can see that the evolution of digital libraries did follow a predictable path. A mix of local, disconnected systems gave way to greater consolidation and investment in protocols that would bring coordination possibilities. Interoperability issues have in recent years received much more significant attention, suggesting a stage of maturity in which "gateways" will ensure coherence. During this evolutionary process, important attention was paid to standards for digital objects and repositories, as well as to the development of a modular architecture that laid important ground for cyberinfrastructure development.

Technology was not the only focus for digital library development. Myriad other issues required critical attention, including issues of user behavior, library organizational structure, professional development, sustainable economic models, governance structures for collaborative efforts, and other social dimensions of digital libraries. An array of evidence suggests that digital libraries are now in a more advanced stage of development. Formal organizations and consortia (e.g., the Digital Library Federation) have been established to further collaboration among institutions. Education and leadership development programs have been established (e.g., the Frye Institute and the transformation of schools of library science into schools of information). Journals have been launched with a focus on digital library issues. These are all markers of a more mature field of activity.

Dan Greenstein and Suzanne Thorin (Greenstein and Thorin 2002) have provided an interesting analysis of digital library infrastructure, using case studies to illustrate the evolutionary path from projects to production environments. Early stages simply extrapolated from traditional library functions (e.g., cataloging expanded to incorporate metadata, and digitization followed practices for microfilming). Greenstein and Thorin noted several salient points that may be generalizable to cyberinfrastructure development. Each digital library they studied was shaped by institutional priorities and strengths. Collaboration with campus information-technology organizations or academic disciplines (e.g., computer or information science) was common, and leadership was essential both from within the library and often from the highest ranks of the university. These elements will be important in cyberinfrastructure development as well.

Perhaps most important, Greenstein and Thorin note the imperative of reconceiving classic library roles and functions and integrating digital practices in the library's repertoire. They write:

> Having acquired core competencies and technical understanding, the maturing digital library abandons the "build it and they will come" philosophy that characterized earlier approaches to collection development. It focuses instead on integrating digital materials into the library's collections and on developing . . . the policies, technical capacities, and professional skills needed to sustain it . . . .
>
> The extent to which libraries are able to realize any part of the grander vision, however, depends almost entirely on their ability to transcend their historic organizational independence and insularity. (Greenstein and Thorin 2002, p. 12)

With this brief history of the foundations of digital libraries, let us now turn to the issues of E-science and research libraries.

North American Research Libraries' E-Science Agenda

Within North America, the ARL is the professional organization that provides leadership for research libraries (123 institutional members in 2008) in the United States and Canada. ARL's mission statement captures its focus on shaping the future of libraries primarily through collaboration with other stakeholders within academe and through information policy development:

> ARL influences the changing environment of scholarly communication and the public policies that affect research libraries and the diverse communities they serve. ARL pursues this mission by advancing the goals of its member research libraries, providing leadership in public and information policy to the scholarly and higher education communities, fostering the exchange of ideas and expertise, and shaping a future environment that leverages its interests with those of allied organizations.[1]

In 2006, ARL's steering committees for Scholarly Communication and Research, Teaching, and Learning jointly charged a task force to deal with the arena of E-science.[2] Specifically, the charge provided a mandate to shape an early agenda for developing E-science capacity within research libraries, including these elements:

- Developing an understanding within the research library community about the issues and needs associated with E-science and cyberinfrastructure and the associated needs of scientists and researchers
- Recommending approaches to addressing issues related to the curation of long-lived digital data, including the handling of simulations and storage of massive data sets
- Engaging ARL members in the development of new roles for libraries as E-science infrastructure and service needs emerge at research institutions
- Identifying the skills needed as information professionals move into the emerging E-science landscape and encouraging the development of information professionals prepared to assume new roles
- Identifying opportunities and recommending strategies for developing relationships with various government scientific agencies and other key stakeholders such as scientific societies

This charge provides a useful framework that will be used here in discussing the challenges for research libraries as requirements emerge for supporting E-science.

Building Understanding of E-Science within Research Libraries

The growing importance of supporting scientific research processes creates a sense of urgency within the library community to better understand what E-science entails and how the library might provide support for the associated tasks, methodologies, and information requirements. Several recent studies have been undertaken to capture the emerging behaviors and interests of the scientific community.[3] In general, these assessments point to a number of hurdles facing scientists that are particularly acute for E-science. The findings of these assessments include the following:

- Research is increasingly interdisciplinary, which is most often defined as scientists with different interests and backgrounds working together as a team on a shared project or problem
- The volume of information makes it difficult to keep current in one's primary discipline, and interdisciplinary fields compound the challenge
- Scientists are experiencing information overload and need information systems that better integrate disparate sources
- Researchers are generating vast amounts of data and having difficulty managing these assets
- Programs and protocols to preserve scientific data are not well developed
- There is increasing need for tools to assist in personal information management
- Mechanisms to sustain communication and involvement across distances of time and space are increasingly important as collaborative science bridges multiple institutions around the globe

These general challenges for contemporary scientists are further stressed by the particular approaches and characteristics of E-science. A recent report, *Towards 2020 Science* (2006), identifies a number of specific attributes of E-science methodologies that are foundational for these new scientific processes:

- Computer science plays a fundamental role within E-science, providing approaches to manage and develop theory, data, and experimentation. The development of computational methodologies and "computational thinking" are key characteristics of E-science.
- E-science integrates theory, experiments, and models. Modeling is a critical tool, linking the data and experimentation.
- Sophisticated frameworks are essential to incorporate the data, models, and complex relationships between these components.
- E-science involves the codification of knowledge—that is, "turning knowledge into a coded representation, in terms of data or programs that are mechanically executable and analyzable" (*Towards 2020 Science*, 2006, 30).
- Software development is central to E-science. Software is necessary to manage and share data, and software is essential in the construction of analyses and synthesis of the data.
- The processes of E-science involve complex work flows that may comprise thousands of steps of computation and data analysis (this issue was the subject of an NSF Workshop on the Challenges of Scientific Workflows, 2006).

These characteristics of E-science methodologies underscore the importance of data, data models, and sophisticated work flows. Each of these interrelated components requires documentation and management. As a first step in developing broader understanding of these methodologies and characteristics, the ARL Task Force recommended an educational campaign targeting both library directors and science librarians. Panels at ARL membership meetings in 2008 featured scientists from major E-science communities and also the Science Commons. A forum jointly sponsored with the Coalition for Networked Information in fall 2008 analyzed the changing requirements for science libraries to serve the scientific community. Speakers explored specific project models, technologies for virtual communities, as well as federal funding agency priorities (Association of Research Libraries 2008).

Data Collections: Preservation, Curation, Management

Given the sheer volume and complexity of scientific data, issues associated with data management and preservation are some of the most vexing and have already received considerable attention. In 2005, NSF sponsored two workshops devoted to data, and the resulting report, *Long-Lived Digital Data Collections* (National Science Foundation 2005), provides a detailed overview of issues associated with data collections, roles and responsibilities of stakeholders, and relevant policy.

The NSF report includes useful definitions of the three primary categories of data collections: *research* database collections, which are specific to a single investigator or research project; *resource* or *community* database collections, which have intermediate-sized user communities and may require longer availability; and *reference* collections, which are managed for long-term use by many users. Data may also be distinguished by their type—that is, whether they are observational, computational (resulting from executing a computer model or simulation), or experimental. Observational and experimental data may not be replicable and, therefore, may carry particular importance for long-term preservation. The process of science also creates derivative data. Each of these categories may carry different requirements for data stewardship.

In 2006, the ARL received funding from NSF to convene a workshop to address issues associated with roles and responsibilities of data stewardship. The workshop brought together librarians and scientists, including representatives from several data-intensive programs. The resulting report, *To Stand the Test of Time: Long-term Stewardship of Digital Data Sets in Science and Engineering* (Association of Research Libraries 2006), explores the potential roles of libraries in managing and preserving data. More specific definitions of roles are articulated in this report, making important distinctions between functions:

- Stewardship of data involves both preservation and curation
- Data preservation involves management practices and long-term care of the data
- Data curation involves ways of organizing, displaying, and repurposing preserved data collections (Association of Research Libraries 2006, 18)

It is worth noting that libraries could be engaged in preservation, curation, or both.

The ARL workshop also underscored the complexities introduced by the unprecedented size of data sets, the discipline-specific data models that are required, and difficulties of identifying a sustainable economic model for long-term preservation of data. Given the interdisciplinary focus, E-science often draws on data from multiple sources and often the data are collected for another purpose; consequently systems to repurpose data and to enable interoperability between data sets are critical. These requirements demand robust metadata schema, ontologies to describe the relationship of data and associated elements in the scientific work flow, and documentation of data models employed.

While this paper cannot address all of these issues in detail, the grand challenges of data described above suggest roles in which libraries do have a base of experience that will need to be significantly stretched. Moving the library from techniques for managing digital objects and associated metadata to involvement in documenting data models, ontologies, and work flow goes well beyond the current library repertoire of description and preservation of information resources.

The final recommendations of the ARL workshop focused on six key areas for NSF investment. Funding was recommended for (1) projects that would develop practices for data ingest, archiving, and re-use; (2) training and development of library and other professionals to support data curation and preservation; (3) the development of usable and useful tools to assist in manipulating digital data; (4) developing sustainable economic models for data stewardship; (5) requirements for data management plans as part of future grant submissions; and (6) the development of national data sharing policies. The first three areas have obvious implications for libraries. Also, to the extent to which libraries become involved in data preservation and curation, they may be called upon to assist scientists in preparing data management plans. Libraries' continued role in providing access to information may logically extend to the development of an overall framework to document the existence of data and to services that assist researchers in finding and using relevant data sources.

Anticipated NSF funding for collaborative data projects and centers could provide research libraries with opportunities for early participation in the development of data practices and models.

In addition to issues of data preservation and curation, there is a logical relationship to be forged between data and the resulting publication of research results. The relationship of data to traditional processes of scholarly communication is an important area for library attention. We already have examples of electronic journals that provide links to the underlying and associated data. There are also examples where the data associated with a journal article are actually actionable; that is, they are in a form such that computational analysis can be executed directly. Some projections, however, foresee far richer relationships between these components of the scientific communication process:

> Yet, far from limiting themselves to merely linking to databases, scientific journals will in some senses need to become databases. Initially this will manifest itself in the way that papers handle accompanying data sets. In the longer term, though, hybrid publications will emerge that combine the strengths of traditional journals with those of databases.

We are likely to see a new breed of scientific publication emerge on a timescale of about 10 years that will cater primarily to researchers who wish to publish valuable scientific data for others to analyse. The data will be peer-reviewed and the author will get credit for having published a paper even if the information contained does not explicitly present any new scientific insights. (*Towards 2020 Science* 2006, 19)

This concept of integrated journal articles and data will require libraries to develop new, integrated methods of description and access. Jane Hunter (2006), for example, has described an approach to encapsulating data, derived products, algorithms, software, and textual publications within "scientific publication packages." These packages provide important information about the lineage of the data and the relationships between the components of the publication.

One final comment on data policies is particularly relevant to libraries. Just as the open-access movement has prompted libraries to engage in policy discussions about open and sustainable access to scientific journal literature, so, too, the open-data movement will prompt libraries to understand the implications and advantages of models that encourage unfettered access to data, where appropriate. Efforts are also taking shape through programs such as the Science Commons[4] to provide licensing models that remove barriers to the sharing of information, tools, and data within the scientific research cycle.

Virtual Organizations: A New Model of Support

One of NSF's priority areas for investment is in the development of virtual organizations. There is the expectation that researchers, distributed across multiple organizations, will convene to work on specific scientific problems and will require online environments that integrate communication technologies, relevant information and data sources, documented work flows, and access to relevant hardware, software, and instrumentation. These types of "collaboratories," as they are sometimes called, present interesting opportunities for libraries. To include relevant information sources, collaboratories will likely draw on licensed library resources, and mechanisms to ensure access across multiple institutions and multiple licenses will be necessary. Additionally, however, libraries are challenged to define roles within these virtual organizations that build on library expertise in the information environment.

Library involvement with digital repositories provides one area that might lend itself to the evolution of virtual organizations. Discipline-focused repositories could provide an important, core component for the virtual organization to which relevant social tools for collaboration could be added. Other potential components were cited above in the inventories of behavioral assessment studies.[5] Scientists require tools to manage their personal research information, and services to provide timely updates about new, relevant information. Libraries are already engaged in both of these areas and can bring this expertise to the emerging virtual organizations. Given the modular architectures that have evolved for digital libraries, libraries also have experience in integrating component service with other online services.

The successful development of virtual organizations will also require attention to the social and cultural issues that might hinder the coordination of activities within complex organizations of researchers, tools, and data. Clifford Lynch eloquently describes the challenge and the rich potential for libraries:

> From one perspective, these [virtual] environments are natural extensions of digital library environments, but at least some sectors of the digital library community have always found active work environments to be an uncomfortable fit with the rather passive tradition of libraries; perhaps here the baggage of "digital libraries" as the disciplinary frame is less than helpful. But there is a rich research agenda that connects literatures and evidence with authoring, analysis and re-use in a much more comprehensive way than we have done to date; this would consider, for example, the interactions between the practices of scholarly authoring and communication on one hand, and on the other, the shifting practices of scholarship that are being recognized and accelerated by investments in e-science and e-research. (Lynch 2005)

New Roles and Skills for Library Professionals

In this discussion of the characteristics and activities of E-science, there have been a number of examples of how libraries and librarians could play a role. Obviously, the identification, dissemination, and management of the scientific literature remain as critical components of science. In addition, there is the potential that library professionals will bring expertise associated with content management and preservation to the arena of data stewardship, stretching existing skills to meet more complex requirements for description and access. And as traditional science publication is transformed to integrate text, data, models, and more, the library will be challenged to develop appropriate description and access for these compound objects. The service roles of libraries are also likely to be sustained and to grow in the online information environment, with the additional complexity of serving distributed and virtual communities of users. As this list suggests, the classic roles of libraries—developing and preserving collections, developing access schema, and developing services to meet information needs—provide an important base from which to develop roles in E-science.

The relatively recent development of digital libraries has also provided the library community with important expertise and experience. As described in an earlier section of this paper, digital library development stretched the classic roles of libraries and forged relationships with computer scientists and information technologists, both important for the continued agenda for applied research and development. The specialized expertise that digital library requirements have created has also prompted new types of positions—e.g., for Web services, metadata creation, interface design, and digital content management.

In order to develop sufficient depth of expertise to serve E-science, we will see increasing attention to training and development. NSF, for example, has a program to foster the development of current and future generations of scientists to develop cyber-based tools and environments. The Institute of Museum and Library Services has similarly provided support for new curricula within information science programs to address the needs of E-science. The complexities of E-science and discipline-specific methodologies make it highly likely that discipline-domain expertise will also be critical to successful library involvement.

The UK's Digital Curation Center (DCC) has a significant track record in professional development, and its suite of programs and training opportunities are indicative of the emerging needs. For example, recent program offerings include specialized professional development workshops addressing persistent identifiers, digital repositories, costing models for digital curation, and legal considerations.[6] Similarly, the University of Illinois Graduate School of Library and Information Science has recently announced course offerings in informatics, data curation, and information modeling.

Resources to support the continuing education of the library community around these issues will also be necessary. The DCC provides an excellent model for the profession with its role in managing a site with rich resources. Further, the DCC is taking a lead role in developing reference publications, including a digital-curation manual[7] with commissioned installments covering topics ranging from archiving to work flow, from ontologies to file formats.

As the library community becomes more engaged in E-science, we are also likely to see the emergence of specialized positions that will build on existing digital library skills, but focus particularly on building the library's role in E-science. Some have argued that the past evolution of positions within the medical library community offers a relevant case study. Within that community there have been clinical librarian positions that involved the librarian as a member of the medical team for patient care. A later iteration on this theme engaged the librarian as a member of a campus enterprise information systems team. Finally, more recent "informationist" positions bring subject domain expertise into the research context, with a focus on developing services and tools to serve the clinical and research communities (Giuse et al. 2005).

The next few years will undoubtedly bring increasing library investment to these issues of professional development and specialization, with critical early support coming from grants and institutional strategic investments. In the longer term, we can expect that support will require reallocation of resources within library organizations, similar to earlier adaptations to changing needs and priorities.

Relationships between Stakeholder Communities

The final area of foundational investment for the research libraries comes in the form of networking and building relationships with relevant stakeholder communities. In including this priority in the charge to the E-Science Task Force, ARL recognized the imperative of joining forces with discipline-based organizations, with government agencies, and with scholarly societies and associations. These collaborations will bring richer and more coordinated attention to the challenges of E-science and the associated policy landscape.

Given the potential for commercial support and involvement in areas of E-science, including existing publisher investment, public-private partnerships can be anticipated.

This will bring an additional dimension of complexity to the ongoing management of, and provision of access to, the assets produced and sustained within the E-science community. As noted above, the research community will need to be vigilant about the academic values associated with access to research resources.

Given the diversity of stakeholders in E-science, collaboration will be a critical strategy for developing cyberinfrastructure. This includes collaboration within institutions, across institutional boundaries, and between public and private sectors. Collaboration brings challenges, particularly in understanding the requirements for working in a virtual context. These challenges warrant attention and the development of models to document expectations of the stakeholders as well as the commitments to levels of services. Fran Berman and colleagues (2007) have provided a useful case study that explores the development of formal agreements necessary to sustain relationships among stakeholders and also the commitments necessary to build trust among participants.

Concluding Remarks

In some respects, the challenges of E-science bear remarkable similarity to those that came to the fore as digital libraries took shape. The requirements for digital library infrastructure prompted investments in understanding and developing technologies, in building organizational capacity, and in forging strategic relationships within the library community and with allied organizations and stakeholders. These relatively recent developments in digital libraries have laid important groundwork for E-science, building foundational architecture as well as essential digital content.

While E-science will build on what we have learned and developed within the digital library landscape, it will also raise new challenges. The inherently interdisciplinary and multi-institutional focus will prompt libraries to consider new paradigms for providing content and services. The complexities of computationally driven and data-intensive science will demand collaboration with computer science and a more intimate engagement with the work flow of disciplinary domains of science. The necessary cyberinfrastructure will require significant retooling of professional skills and ongoing investment in continuing education.

The foray into E-science will also encourage each research library to work collaboratively with other research libraries as the network of E-science and cyberinfrastructure is created. These collaborations will be within particular E-science projects and more broadly within the research library community as policy and applied research developments unfold.

E-science presents us with both unprecedented challenge and unprecedented opportunity. The potential for libraries and librarians as critical components in virtual organizations suggests a diffuse and strategic role for libraries that could be essential to the success of E-science in this century. The next decade will bring important investment in building alliances, infrastructure, and expertise to realize this strategic agenda.

Notes

NB: Internet addresses in the text, the notes, and the references were accurate as of December 23, 2008.

1. http://www.arl.org/arl/governance/mission.shtml.
2. http://www.arl.org/rtl/escience/escicharge.shtml.
3. *Researchers and Discovery Services: Behaviour, Perceptions and Needs.* Study commissioned by the Research Information Network. November 2006. http://www.rin.ac.uk/files/Report%20-%20final.pdf; "Biosciences Resources and Services Planning" at the University of Washington. 2007. Summary at http://www.cni.org/tfms/2007a.spring/abstracts/PB-faculty-persily.html; *Supporting the Research Needs of Scientists: A University of Minnesota Libraries Study.* September 2005 to June 2007. http://www2.lib.umn.edu/about/scieval/.
4. http://sciencecommons.org.
5. *Researchers and Discovery Services*; "Biosciences Resources and Services Planning"; *Supporting the Research Needs of Scientists.*
6. http://www.dcc.ac.uk/.
7. http://www.dcc.ac.uk/resource/curation-manual/.

References

Association of Research Libraries. 2006. *To Stand the Test of Time: Long-Term Stewardship of Digital Data Sets in Science and Engineering.* Arlington, VA, September 26–27. http://www.arl.org/bm~doc/digdatarpt.pdf.

Association of Research Libraries. 2008. *Reinventing Science Librarianship: Models for the Future.* ARL/CNI Fall Forum, Arlington, VA, October. http://www.arl.org/resources/pubs/fallforumproceedings/forum08proceedings.shtml.

Berghel, Hal. 2001. "Digital Village: A Cyberpublishing Manifesto." *Communications of the ACM* 44, no. 3 (March): 17–20.

Berman, Fran, Robert H. McDonald, Brian E. C. Schottlaender, and Ardys Kozbial. 2007. The Need for Formalized Trust in Digital Repository Collaborative Infrastructure. NSF/JISC repositories workshop, April 16. http://www.sis.pitt.edu/~repwkshop/papers/berman_schottlaender.html.

Edwards, Paul N., Steven J. Jackson, Geoffrey C. Bowker, and Cory P. Knobel. 2007. Understanding Infrastructure: Dynamics, Tensions, and Design. Report of a Workshop on History & Theory of Infrastructure: Lessons for New Scientific Cyberinfrastructures. January. http://www.si.umich.edu/cyber-infrastructure/UnderstandingInfrastructure_FinalReport25jan07.pdf.

Giuse, Nunzia B., Taneya Y. Koonce, Rebecca N. Jerome, Molynda Cahall, Nila A. Sathe, and Annette Williams. 2005. "Evolution of a Mature Clinical Informationist Model." *Journal of the American Medical Informatics Association* 12, no. 3 (May/June): 249–55.

Greenstein, Daniel, and Suzanne E. Thorin. 2002. *The Digital Library: A Biography.* Digital Library Federation, Council on Library and Information Resources. http://www.clir.org/pubs/reports/pub109/pub109.pdf.

Hey, Tony, and Jessie Hey. 2006. "E-Science and Its Implications for the Library Community." *Library Hi Tech* 24, no. 4: 515–28.

Hunter, Jane. 2006. "Scientific Publication Packages—A Selective Approach to the Communica-
     tion and Archival [*sic*] of Scientific Output." *International Journal of Digital Curation* 1, no. 1
     (Autumn): 33–52. http://www.ijdc.net/index.php/ijdc/article/viewFile/8/4.

Lawrence, Katherine A., Thomas A. Finholt, and Il-hwan Kim. 2007. "Warm Fronts and
     High Pressure Systems: Overcoming Geographic Dispersion in a Meteorological Cyberin-
     frastructure Project." Proceedings of the 40th Annual Hawaii International Conference on
     System Sciences, 1–10. http://www.crew.umich.edu/publications/tr_07_08.html.

Lynch, Clifford. 2005. "Where Do We Go from Here? The Next Decade for Digital Libra-
     ries." *D-Lib Magazine* 11, no. 7/8 (July/August). http://www.dlib.org/dlib/july05/lynch/
     07lynch.html.

National Science Foundation, Blue-Ribbon Advisory Panel on Cyberinfrastructure.
     2003. *Revolutionizing Science and Engineering through Cyberinfrastructure.* http://
     www.communitytechnology.org/nsf_ci_report/.

National Science Foundation. National Science Board. 2005. *Long-Lived Digital Data Collec-
     tions: Enabling Research and Education in the 21st Century.* http://www.nsf.gov/pubs/2005/
     nsb0540/nsb0540.pdf.

National Science Foundation. 2006. Workshop on the Challenges of Scientific Workflows.
     Arlington, VA, May 1–2. http://vtcpc.isi.edu/wiki/index.php/Main_Page.

National Science Foundation. Cyberinfrastructure Council. 2007. *Cyberinfrastructure Vision
     for 21st Century Discovery.* http://www.nsf.gov/pubs/2007/nsf0728/index.jsp.

Taylor, John. 2005. E-Research—Col-laboratories [*sic*] and Curation. E-research Open
     Forum, Canberra, Australia, September 20. http://epp.ph.unimelb.edu.au/twiki/pub/
     EPPGrid/EResearchPage/SirJohnTaylorPresentationCanberra.pdf.

Towards 2020 Science. 2006. Microsoft Research. http://research.microsoft.com/towards2020
     science/downloads.htm.

CHAPTER 3

THE CHALLENGES OF E-SCIENCE DATA SET MANAGEMENT AND SCHOLARLY COMMUNICATION FOR DOMAIN SCIENCES AND ENGINEERING: A ROLE FOR ACADEMIC LIBRARIES AND LIBRARIANS

James L. Mullins

Abstract

The challenge of accessing, maintaining, sharing, and preserving massive data sets, generally referred to as data curation, has been a direct result of computational E-science. Although scientists and engineers have recognized the problem, the solution has not been apparent. The principles that underlie library science are not widely understood or appreciated by those outside librarianship. The theory and principles behind librarianship are obscured by historical application primarily to print materials—books and journals. However, the same principles that apply to organization, retrieval, and preservation of print materials apply to the digital realm as well.

The National Science Foundation (NSF) in the United States is concerned that much of its funding has been committed to creating data sets, used for specific research projects and then discarded. The question is, couldn't a data set be "mined" for more than one research project? The NSF has begun to assess and research the issues associated with "archiving" data sets for present and future research use.

What are the challenges faced by the sciences in managing massive data sets? First, this chapter will explore the underlying principles in play to create and archive data. Second, specific data-management applications will be reviewed for clues to the challenge confronting scientists, engineers, computer scientists, information technologists, and librarians to archive and to curate data for present use and, ultimately, for use far into the future.

Introduction

The research role of university libraries and librarians is changing. With the ever-increasing need to manage massive digital data sets by domain researchers, opportunities for new collaboration are developing between the disciplinary researchers in science, engineering, and technology and a newly found colleague, the librarian. Challenges faced by researchers in organizing and accessing massive data sets have created the need for, and a new appreciation of, the training and knowledge of librarians. The opportunity for librarians to participate as co-investigators in sponsored/funded research is increasing.

A 2005 report from the U.S. National Science Board (NSB), *Long-Lived Digital Data Collections Enabling Research and Education in the 21st Century,* confirmed this crisis in data management and called for the creation of new research positions that closely replicate the professional knowledge of librarians.[1] The positions of data manager and data scientist, as described in the report, have important elements that the education and experience of librarians fulfill.

A National and International Challenge

From where has this need come? It is the basis for much of what E-science is about. What exactly qualifies as E-science? For that we need to review an accepted definition as provided by the United Kingdom's "e-Science Programme":

> What is meant by e-Science? In the future, e-Science will refer to the large scale science that will increasingly be carried out through distributed global collaborations enabled by the Internet. Typically, a feature of such collaborative scientific enterprises is that they will require access to very large data collections, very large scale computing resources and high performance visualization back to the individual user scientists.[2]

What is the scale that is being proposed and discussed here? It can range from a few gigabytes to the creation of 30 terabytes of data every day. An example of an E-science project that is now being planned and developed is the Large Synoptic Survey Telescope (LSST). The 8.4 m LSST, to be located in Peru, is a wide-field telescope facility that will provide new capabilities in astronomy. The LSST will provide time-lapse digital imaging of faint astronomical objects across the entire sky. The LSST has been identified as a national scientific priority in reports by diverse U.S. and international panels, including several National Academy of Sciences and federal agency advisory committees. This judgment is based on the LSST's ability to address some of the most pressing open questions in astronomy and fundamental physics, while driving advances in data-intensive science and computing.[3]

The current estimate for the LSST's data generation is 36 gigabytes (GB) of data every 30 seconds; thereby, over a 10-hour night the scan will generate approximately 30 terabytes of data. Within 10 years it is estimated that the LSST will require computational power at the rate of nearly 100 teraflops.

Does the LSST project represent the largest computation projected? Only time will tell. Mapping the universe, the earth, the atmosphere, plant and animal genomes, all this will generate massive amounts of data, requiring computational power, storage, and curation.

Curation—the Role of Libraries and Librarians

The NSB, beginning on page 25 in the third chapter of its previously mentioned report on *Long-Lived Digital Data Collections*, described the roles and responsibilities of individuals and institutions in data management.[4] The individual roles that are most relevant to this chapter are those of data authors, data managers, and data scientists. In simple terms these three roles break down as follows:

- *Data authors* are domain scientists, educators, and students who have a vested interest in the research generated from the data.

- *Data managers* are information technologists, computer scientists, and information scientists responsible for the computing, storing, and accessing of the data for analysis.

- And *data scientists* are curators, expert annotators, librarians, and archivists, among others. The data scientists have responsibility for undertaking creative inquiry and analysis to enhance the undertaking of research by the data authors, and to apply a consistent methodology and best practices to the curation of data.

As a follow-up to the *Long-lived Digital Data Collections* report, the Association of Research Libraries (ARL), with a grant from the NSF, brought together around 30 individuals to discuss the issues of long-term data stewardship. The workshop, held September 26–27, 2006, in Arlington, Virginia, brought together domain scientists, engineers, computer scientists, information technologists, librarians, and members of NSF and ARL staff. The culmination of the workshop was a report issued in the fall of 2007, entitled *To Stand the Test of Time: Long-term Stewardship of Digital Data Sets in Science and Engineering.*[5]

What is *curation of data*? As with many words, the word *curation* means different things within different fields and professions. *Curation* to a scientist or engineer could be defined as one who "works to identify, classify, analyze and index information . . . The scientific curator enters information into the appropriate databases and keeps written information, reports, case files and necessary documentation."[6] However, to a librarian/archivist, *curation of data* means to store, provide access, preserve, and carry forward data into the future with assurance that the data will be accessible and retrievable for future verification or use. Although the definitions are not overly different, it does require an awareness of this difference in definition to foster conversations between a scientist/engineer and a data scientist (librarian/archivist).

So how is the specialized knowledge of a librarian/archivist applied to the needs of scientific inquiry by the curation of data sets? For hundreds (possibly thousands) of years, people have been designated to organize collections of objects, whether they were papyrus scrolls, cuneiform tablets, vellum manuscripts, or early codex volumes.

In order to locate a particular piece of information, a person or group of people worked together to devise a logical order and structure, a retrieval system methodology, that would assign and locate all materials within the "library." The organizational scheme might serve only one repository (library/archives) or a group for an entire region, generating a consistency and ease of retrieval among distributed researchers. However, it wasn't until the late nineteenth century with the proliferation of publications—books, periodicals, magazines, newspapers—that a standardized approach was necessary. Professional library education developed in the mid-nineteenth century. Soon thereafter professional codes arose for organizing materials, first within a library, such as the Library of Congress classification scheme, and then more universally, such as the Dewey Decimal System. In order to reflect a more international approach (away from practices within the United States), the Colon Classification scheme was developed by Shiyali Ramamrita Ranganathan in 1931 in India.

Cataloging rules were created by the American Library Association in collaboration with the Library Association in Britain in the late-nineteenth century to describe the format and subject of books and periodicals. The cataloging rules (which equate today to metadata) and subject headings (which equate today to taxonomies) organized materials and made them accessible within libraries, while providing a consistent framework that allowed scholars to move from one library to another, knowing that materials would be organized and retrievable in a consistent manner.

Toward the end of the nineteenth century, researchers realized that order must come to the proliferation of professional journals that were being published within the subject domains: chemistry, physics, philosophy, geology, etc. Indexing/abstracting services were started that provided links from authors to articles and to subject content, thereby simplifying researcher access.

In the late-twentieth century the advent and application of computer technology provided remote access initially to automated catalogs and subsequently to digital indexes and abstracts. Much of the research generated today is published in both print and digital format and, more and more, research is being disseminated without even appearing in print. One result of this digital transformation has been that researchers want to be able to "work backwards" from the reported research findings to the underlying data set used in the research. The published research article itself becomes "metadata par excellence" to the underlying data set.

Dr. Christopher Greer, former program director of the Office of Cyberinfrastructure, U.S. NSF, has developed a pentagram that represents the role of the library in the future of data curation within the larger field of E-science. In order to break down perceptions or stereotypes of the role of a library, he places what he refers to as the "I-Center" in the middle of the pentagram with the five surrounding points identified as domain science, computer science, library/information science, archival science, and cyberinfrastructure. His contention is that it will require all five of these specialties to collaborate to develop a model that will be practical and workable to curate the massive data sets that are now being generated.[7]

Several of the points of the pentagram are logical: domain science, computer science, and cyberinfrastructure. It is doubtful that anyone would disagree with these as necessary or critical components. However, how do library/information science and archival science figure in, and why are they separate?

What is *library science*? The typical definition describes *library science* as the practice of administering a library. However, there are more descriptive definitions that define *library science*; for example: "the systematic study and analysis of the sources, development, collection, organization, dissemination, evaluation, use, and management of information in all its forms, including the channels (formal and informal) and technology used in its communication."[8] This definition allows a conceptualization of the theory and principles behind librarianship that the more prosaic definition does not. Therefore, using the definition above, it is apparent that the library as the I-Center can apply the principles and theories of library science, first, by analyzing and understanding the data sources created by the domain scientists, then creating an organizational structure and retrieval points through the application of metadata and taxonomies/ontologies, which will facilitate the dissemination of the data, and finally, by establishing standards for the preservation and archiving of the data.

Librarians are logical as collaborators in this aspect of data curation and management. However, there are two necessary aspects of the curation of data that library science is not prepared to deal with particularly well, and in fact, they fly in the face of the principles of librarianship (information for all, any time, and any place). This is where archival science comes into play. As defined by the Society of American Archivists, "archival science is a systematic body of theory that supports the practice of appraising, acquiring, authenticating, preserving, and providing access to recorded materials."[9] Anyone who works in archives becomes familiar with the "gift terms" of a donor. Often a donor of personal papers will restrict for a period of time who can be provided access to the papers, and the terms are agreed upon and followed. Confidential material can be withheld upon the request of the donor for a specified time, or access can be restricted to a particular group. Additionally, archivists are trained to evaluate massive amounts of paper files, and to retain "examples" rather than the entire collection for the sake of space limitations and timely access. Although archivists rarely deaccession materials, there are times when collections may be weeded or lent to another institution for "contributory collection building." However, the major difference between a librarian's responsibility and that of an archivist is that most often the archivist is handling one-of-a-kind, original materials. *Archives* could be defined as repositories of data, historically in printed form, that, until a researcher (most often a humanist or social scientist) comes to "mine" the materials, are nothing but bits of raw data, not that dissimilar from massive digital data sets that the scientist will mine.

The five points on the I-Center pentagram come together this way: Domain scientists develop a problem, then collect data into a data set to observe, experiment, and develop a conclusion. The data set is housed and made accessible through software written by a computer scientist. Analysis of the data is undertaken and the results are shared through the technology infrastructure. General database access and taxonomic/ontological structure are developed by library scientists through use of metadata and classification designation. Access control and review are managed through archival science. Through this collaboration, the investment of funding agencies, and the time committed by the domain scientists, there is greater assurance that the data will be more generally available today and in the future.

Examples of Data Set Development and Processing

In order to understand the challenges better than we can in an abstract discussion, let us consider the following specific examples. They come from Purdue University, but that does not mean that we at Purdue have a better understanding than others of issues associated with data set creation and curation. Rather, using our own examples simply enables us to draw upon explorations of issues with researchers whom we have met. Moreover, the Purdue examples provide insight into the distributed nature of the need for data curation, the need for data set management internationally, and changes in the scholarly communication paradigm.

Large Synoptic Survey Telescope and Antimatter

Earlier in this chapter the LSST was briefly discussed as a planned endeavor that would ultimately generate massive amounts of data for researchers to mine for insights into the universe through astronomy and astrophysics. One such researcher is Dr. Ian Shipsey, Julian Schwinger distinguished professor of physics, Purdue University. As a particle physicist he accepts that matter comes in pairs; for every kind of particle there is an antiparticle that is identical in mass but differs in other characteristics such as electric charge.[10]

However, though the observable universe is comprised of matter, there is no evidence of antimatter. Dr. Shipsey wants to understand how this asymmetry can exist contrary to the laws of nature. Through the LSST project he will have a massive amount of data gathered nightly to mine and study to possibly unlock the mystery or at least point the way. In order to pursue this research, however, massive amounts of data will need to be sifted, selected, and archived for analysis and future comparisons. How to organize, retrieve, and archive this data will be a challenge. Will this work be undertaken within his lab, independent of other researchers in the field, and without collaboration from computer scientists and information technologists? Very doubtful. But, who will provide guidance for establishing an accepted taxonomy within astrophysics or astronomy to a specific protocol for tagging and linking data for present-day retrieval and long-term future access? Could this be done through the application of library science?

Plant Genetics and The Arabidopsis Information Resource (TAIR)

Dr. David Salt is the scientific director of the Bindley Bioscience Center for Genomic Research and Technology, Discovery Park, and professor of horticulture and landscape architecture, Purdue University. Dr. Salt states in his biographical sketch that "natural variation is well documented in plants, and plants provide an excellent model for investigations into its genetic origins, maintenance, and adaptive significance."[11]

The genetic model plant *Arabidopsis thaliana* can be used to derive the factors that drive the fixation of locally adaptive genetic variation within a population.[12] By identifying the genes and gene networks that control the elemental profile or "ionome" using genetic mapping tools, it will be possible to shed light on the evolutionary processes involved in the adaptation of organisms to local environments. This research is important to mankind since understanding the means by which plants accumulate minerals from the soil is critical for both agriculture and human nutrition. Improvements in our knowledge of this area could have significant impacts on improving nutrition and health standards throughout the world. In order to screen and analyze thousands of *Arabidopsis* samples for their elemental profiles, samples are gathered, processed, and tracked. Each sample has 18 elements identified and quantified, and the concentration of each element is compared to a standard norm.

Database and middleware applications were written within Dr. Salt's lab that allow for efficient and consistent transfer of metadata and analytical data for each sample. Through the metadata the sample is identified and stored in a local database. Metadata is also used to index the analytical data to the TAIR database.[13] The software provides a public interface to allow data search, visualization, and download.

Although currently the software is available for use only within the Purdue Ionomics Information Management System (PiiMS), Dr. Salt wishes to make it available as open source to the research community. When asked whether the data being collected and stored in PiiMS and in TAIR would be useful and needed in 30, 50, 100 years, his response was, "Yes, definitely, you might as well be asking whether the human genome information would be useful in one hundred years!"[14]

Nanotechnology—the Latest Frontier

Nanotechnology has become the latest developing research area, requiring considerable interdisciplinary collaboration. In order to facilitate learning and discovery in nanotechnology, it is critical that information be exchanged and data shared, stored, and archived. A major effort of this kind is the nanoHUB, a project supported by the Network for Computational Nanotechnology (NCN), whose funding is received from the NSF. Although the nanoHUB does not include the storage and curation of massive data sets, it is included in this paper as an example of an information exchange, not dissimilar to what has typically been thought of as the role of a research library. Interesting insights can be gained by looking at the role nanoHUB plays in collecting and sharing information in nanotechnology. What is the present and future role for centers such as nanoHUB and their relationship to libraries? Who has the responsibility to preserve the record of scholarly communication as generated by information and research exchanges such as the nanoHUB?

In order to understand the thrust of nanotechnology, it may be helpful to review its definition. *Nanotechnology* is defined on the home page of the nanoHUB as follows:

A nanometer is one-billionth of a meter—25,000 times smaller than the width of a human hair, 200 times smaller than a typical virus, about the size of 3–4 atoms laid end-to-end. At that tiny scale, matter can exhibit some strange, new behaviors. Nano-technology is all about harnessing those behaviors to create new devices and materials. Imagine a new material that is 100 times stronger than steel, with only one-sixth the weight! Imagine making a transistor out of a single molecule! Imagine molecular machines that practice personalized nanomedicine by repairing damaged cells. These are still dreams, but scientists and engineers in laboratories all over the world are working to make these dreams a reality—to turn the promise of nanoscience into technologies for the benefit of human society.[15]

Therefore, to link researchers throughout the world who are studying the property of a nanometer and its application to furthering science is critical. The mission of the nanoHUB as provided on its Web site is as follows:

The nanoHUB, a web-based resource for research, education, and collaboration in nano-technology, is an initiative of the NSF-funded Network for Computational Nanotech-nology (NCN). The NCN is a network of universities with a vision to pioneer the development of nanotechnology from science to manufacturing through innovative theory, exploratory simulation, and novel cyberinfrastructure. NCN students, staff, and faculty are developing the nanoHUB science gateway while making use of it in their own research and education. Collaborators and partners across the world have joined the NCN in this effort.[16]

The nanoHUB is a resource to the entire nano-community focused on the three themes of the NCN: nanoelectronics, NEMS/nanofluidics, and nanomedicine/biology. The nanoHUB brings together scientists, computer scientists, and applied mathematicians to work through problems and propose solutions and, through this collaborative endeavor, it has become a major information exchange. The following is a brief summary of the information exchange as well as an analysis of success. Although the nanoHUB is used by over 5,000 people doing research each year, the largest numbers of people coming to the nanoHUB are looking for educational materials: the nanoHUB had over 20,000 total users in 2006.[17]

The nanoHUB provides simulation in nanoelectronics, NEMS/nanofluidics, and nanobio plus other developing tools. The nanoHUB provides research support through links to online seminars, provides links for collaboration and online meet-ings, and facilitates user groups. Through its teach and learn section it provides links to online courses that university students (and researchers) can take to introduce themselves to the study of nanotechnology, and even includes teaching materials on nanotechnology for young children.

The nanoHUB is free for anyone to join. The nanoHUB encourages its commu-nity to participate in the dissemination of content by uploading their own content. The nanoHUB is available throughout the world through the Internet. Simulation set-up and data exploration are interactive, geared toward noncomputing experts. The nanoHUB team estimates, through an evaluation of the offered tools, user surveys, and tool usage, that usage is about one-third for educational purposes, one-third for research purposes, and one-third in a mixed education/research mode.

The scholarly communication that is being facilitated through the nanoHUB is critical in a newly defined field of research. Without the exchange of research findings, simulation modeling, and integration into the curriculum and learning of students from primary school through university, the field would not be advancing as it is. Research and education resources, such as the nanoHUB Nano 501 tutorials as well as research seminars, are finding their way into citations in the research literature. The traditional scholarly communication mode of research publications would likely not meet the real time needs of nanotechnology researchers. Furthermore the nano-HUB is disseminating information in new forms of media such as interactive, voice-over presentations, and PODcasts that can be accessed through iTunes. Therefore, how do libraries assess this new role of information dissemination and integrate it into their responsibilities? Additionally, how do libraries ensure that the record, as it is now being created, is preserved and archived for the future?

Conclusion

Is there a role for librarians and libraries, archivists and archives, in the curation of massive data sets coupled with new methods of scholarly communication in support of E-science? If we look at library and archival science through the principles of information organization, access, retrieval, and preservation, then, yes, there is a clear relationship and role. However, if we continue to view the role of librarians and archivists as passive participants in the "finished" product of research, there is likely only a small, more traditional role to play. As in most prognostications, the reality will likely fall somewhere in between. To define what is expected in the curation of massive data sets and establish the policies and processes necessary to accomplish this will be major challenges for E-science researchers and information specialists for the immediate future and beyond.

Notes

NB: Internet addresses in the following notes were accurate as of January 30, 2009.

1. U.S. National Science Board, *Long-Lived Digital Data Collections Enabling Research and Education in the 21st Century*, NSB-05-40, September 2005, 26–27, http://www.nsf.gov/pubs/2005/nsb0540/.

2. Research Councils UK, e-Science, About the UK e-Science Programme, http://www.rcuk.ac.uk/escience/default.htm.

3. LSST, Large Scale Survey Telescope, The New Sky, http://www.lsst.org/About/lsst_about.shtml.

4. U.S. National Science Board, *Long-Lived Digital Data Collections*.

5. Association of Research Libraries, *To Stand the Test of Time: Long-Term Stewardship of Digital Data Sets in Science and Engineering, a Report to the National Science Foundation from*

the ARL Workshop on New Collaborative Relationships: The Role of Academic Libraries in the Digital Data Universe, September 2006, Arlington, VA.

6. Biohealthmatics.com. *Serving the Biomedical Informatics Community!* http:// www.biohealthmatics.com/careers/PID00305.aspx.

7. Christopher Greer, A Vision for the Digital Data Universe, part of a presentation given at Purdue University, West Lafayette, IN, December 19, 2006.

8. Joan M. Reitz, ODLIS—Online Dictionary for Library and Information Science, http:// lu.com/odlis/search.cfm.

9. Richard Pearce-Moses, A Glossary of Archival and Records Terminology, http:// www.archivists.org/glossary/term_details.asp?DefinitionKey=1814.

10. Ian Shipsey, Matter Antimatter Asymmetry and the Universe, http://www .physics.purdue.edu/~shipsey/research/newsletter/Newsletter.html.

11. David E. Salt, Biographical Sketch, http://www.hort.purdue.edu/hort/NRC/Salt% 20CV%2007.pdf.

12. Ibid.

13. The Arabidopsis Information Resource (TAIR), Ohio State University, 2007, http:// www.arabidopsis.org/index.jsp.

14. Personal interview with David E. Salt, Purdue University, May 15, 2007.

15. nanoHUB, About Us, Network for Computational Nanotechnology, Purdue University, West Lafayette, IN, http://www.nanohub.org/about/.

16. Ibid.

17. nanoHUB, Usage Overview, Network for Computational Nanotechnology, Purdue University, West Lafayette, IN, http://www.nanohub.org/usage/.

CHAPTER 4

Changes in Research Libraries as a Result of E-Science Initiatives: A Snapshot

Neil Rambo

0. Contents

1. Introduction

2. ARL Joint Task Force on Library Support for E-science

3. Implications for Libraries

4. Changes in U.S. Research Libraries in Response to E-science

5. Related Changes and Other Initiatives

6. Conclusion

7. References

8. Appendix A: ARL E-Science Task Force Members

9. Appendix B: ARL E-Science Task Force Recommendations

1. Introduction

In chapter two of this book, Wendy Pradt Lougee described E-science as an emerging research methodology and argued that this development has enormous implications for research libraries. E-science can be thought of as a fourth research methodology, added to the standard ways of knowing through theory, experiment, and observation. This methodology is characterized as driven by networked capabilities and vast amounts of data. Hey and Hey note that well-established experimental and theoretical methodologies have been stretched in recent decades by computational methods, and now an era of large-scale, data-driven, and computationally intense science is rapidly taking shape (Hey and Hey 2006). As Lougee observed, E-science fundamentally alters the ways in which scientists interact, the tools they employ, the types of problems they address, and the nature of the documentation and publication that results from their research.

Lougee stated that E-science requires new strategies for research support and significant development of infrastructure. She outlined how fundamental aspects of the research library's functions and roles are influenced by these new methodologies. Libraries have traditionally been structured and staffed around disciplines, yet E-science embraces a multidisciplinary approach. E-science is dependent on computational resources and services, but libraries' computational involvements are modest in comparison. E-science is data-intensive, yet libraries have generally not collected or managed and preserved scientific data. E-science is typically conducted in a team context, often spanning multiple institutions and national boundaries. But libraries are oriented toward a primary user constituency affiliated with a single institution. Correspondingly, use licenses governing online content and the infrastructure for authentication and authorization do not translate well to a multi-institutional environment.

These observations led the Association of Research Libraries (ARL) to sponsor an effort to investigate the implications of E-science for research libraries and to recommend a course of action for the library community to pursue. Using that effort and the resulting report as a starting point, I will provide an assessment of the changes that have recently taken place in research libraries due to E-science initiatives. I will conclude with a consideration of trends and likely next steps.

An important caveat for this snapshot is that my focus is on North American research libraries: the membership of the U.S.-based ARL. I am limiting myself to this slice of experience because ARL (and the ARL Task Force) is my connection to this topic and it provides a context with which I am familiar.

It should be noted that this is a significant limitation because there are fewer developments in response to E-science in U.S. (and to some extent Canadian) research libraries than there are in many other parts of the world. Decentralization in the United States makes it extremely difficult to enforce or mandate policies that are closely tied to the progress of E-science; for example, policies on open access and open data. Deep structural differences impede progress in the United States as compared with the European Union, United Kingdom, Australia, and others. I will come back to this point, as well as a few exceptions to it, in section five of this chapter.

2. ARL Joint Task Force on Library Support for E-Science

In 2006, ARL's steering committees for Scholarly Communication and for Research, Teaching, and Learning jointly appointed a task force to address E-science (task force members are listed in Appendix A). The charge of the Joint Task Force on Library Support for E-Science focused on raising awareness and positioning research libraries to be players in this new arena. There was a growing sense that E-science trends, and more broadly, E-research trends, were evolving rapidly and libraries could miss opportunities for contribution and engagement as this form of research evolved.

The charge of the ARL Task Force provides a mandate to shape an early agenda for developing E-science capacity within research libraries. The mandate includes these elements:

- "Develop an understanding within the research library community about the issues and needs associated with E-science and cyberinfrastructure and the associated needs of scientists and researchers.
- "Recommend approaches to addressing issues related to the curation of long-lived digital data, including the handling of simulations and storage of massive data sets.
- "Engage ARL members in the development of new roles for libraries as E-science infrastructure and service needs emerge at research institutions.
- "Identify the skills needed as information professionals move into the emerging E-science landscape, and encourage the development of information professionals prepared to assume new roles.
- "Identify opportunities and recommend strategies for developing relationships with various government science agencies and other stakeholders such as scientific societies." (ARL 2007)

The ARL task force identified desired outcomes that will position the research library community as a significant partner in the development of E-science. The task force report encouraged ARL, and the broader research library community, to partner with allied organizations and stakeholders to explore and shape a broad vision of the research library's role in an ideal E-science infrastructure, at both the institutional and cross-institutional levels.

The report focused on education, policy, and communication with the ARL community about E-science and associated issues. It called for ARL to build member awareness of the sea change that is coming, or is already upon us, as a result of the emergence of E-science, and to ensure that members are knowledgeable about the implications for libraries.

The task force added a cautionary note that approaching these transformational issues from the constrained perspective of current conditions (e.g., established organizational structures, staffing, funding, etc.) will ultimately be insufficient. A broader engagement is called for throughout the research library community, which must consider a fundamental reassessment of the library's role and structure, in effect redefining the research library for a new era.

The purpose of the report and its recommendations was to establish a foundation upon which to build. It was not intended to be a bold manifesto prescribing what research libraries should do or how to forge ahead. Instead, it was a carefully considered call to a community to raise awareness, foster learning, and promote engagement with the respective enterprises within and across our institutions.

The report considered

1. the implications for research practice of E-science,
2. the national and international context for E-science,

3. critical areas for research library engagement, and

4. current library capability to support E-science.

The report concluded with recommendations, desired outcomes, and suggested strategies and actions. To review these, see Appendix B.

3. Implications for Libraries

In a recent article, William Arms from Cornell University cites examples of how researchers, publishers, and librarians are working together on aspects of what he refers to as "cyberscholarship" (Arms 2008). He discusses the National Virtual Observatory, the Entrez search-engine system from the National Center for Biotechnology Information (NCBI), and the Web Lab at Cornell University as examples of cyberscholarship. Arms concludes that the implications for publishers and libraries are profound but the experience to guide developments is scant. Drawing on his work at the Cornell Web Lab, he provides a framework of lessons learned— along with unanswered questions and challenges—which includes the following elements.

Market research (or user assessment) and incremental development: Libraries need to appreciate potential areas of research and the methodologies used by different disciplines.

Organizational implications: There is a shared need to balance between distribution (e.g., data and services) and centralization (coordination of cyberinfrastructure).

Content: The data need to exist! They have to be accessible. Data that cannot be found or accessed cannot be used. The data need to be assembled and be discoverable. Once discovered, the data need to be accessible under reasonable terms and conditions. Data management includes deciding what to select and acquire, and determining what rises to the level of requiring enhanced metadata creation and long-term preservation.

Tools and services: They may be specific to particular domains, but in order to exploit large data sets they need to include application program interfaces (API) and be able to identify and download subcollections of the whole for more in-depth processing and analysis.

High-performance computing: Massive storage units and access to grid technologies may be necessary for some analyses and problems.

Computational limits: Some techniques work well with moderately large digital collections but fail with very large ones. Analytical tools and techniques may not scale and this may limit the questions that can be addressed.

Expertise in managing massive data collections and providing access and analysis will be limited. Where will staff with the necessary skill sets come from? Will they emerge, for example, from partnerships with other university entities, or from the commercial sector?

Arms's lessons and challenges are, in many respects, a restatement, from a researcher's perspective, of the issues and questions raised in the ARL task force report.

Both perspectives are concerned with understanding the needs of researchers, identifying roles, assessing organizational structures and responsiveness, creating and supporting tools and services, and developing the expertise needed to do all this. This echo between the research library and researcher communities provides corroboration that these issues are in fact the proper ones to focus on. The echo does not provide assurance, however, that either community's perspective is complete: experience may teach us that other challenges await us.

Arms makes the point that the primary user of very large digital libraries is the machine—computers, not humans. Obviously this is especially true for very large data sets. His observation points to the need for the development of APIs so that computer programs can interact directly with collections of data sets. He also underscores the need for interoperable, machine-readable description and access points to facilitate deeper machine access and analysis (Arms 2008).

4. Changes in U.S. Research Libraries in Response to E-Science

The ARL task force report was released at the beginning of 2008. There were programs and discussion sessions at the ARL members meeting in May 2008 that were related to E-science issues. In terms of the report, however, it is too early to expect significant changes to have taken place within research libraries. For the following overview of developments and changes, I draw upon knowledge I gained from my role as ARL visiting program officer for library support for research and E-science. This responsibility has provided me with entrée to people who are working in these areas. Through their network I have gained an awareness of who is active and what changes are taking place in research libraries as a result of E-science activities. I make no claim of comprehensiveness, however. What I relate is simply what I am aware of at the time of this writing.

These changes can be categorized quite simply as big, medium, and small. The big changes are in libraries that have made significant organizational changes, involving reallocation of staffing and budget, in an attempt to position themselves to engage more effectively with E-science activities. There are few of these. The small changes involve little institutional commitment or investment, either in terms of budget or staff. There are understandably many more of these because they involve little risk and, coming relatively early in this foreseen process of transformation, this kind of response positions an institution to monitor and assess without costly commitment. Medium changes are somewhere in between in terms of commitment, cost, and risk.

My informal assessment is that most North American research libraries have not made any changes in response to, or in anticipation of, E-science activities or trends. Some have made some small changes. A very few have made medium or big changes. More are quite likely in the "pre-change" or "thinking about it" phase. Those that have made no changes may have had quite legitimate reasons, not just a lack of awareness or inertia. For example, no-change libraries could be at smaller institutions that emphasize the humanities and liberal arts and have less intense sponsored-research environments.

In such institutions, there may be little need to respond to E-science, for now. But, E-scholarship and E-research will be an increasing emphasis in the arts, humanities, and social sciences. So change will come also to liberal arts libraries in which it is not already happening (ACLS 2006).

At the other end of the scale, libraries that have already committed to substantial changes are presumably doing so in response to institutional developments that support or encourage this kind of response. Research libraries are inherently conservative institutions. Taking high risks and making big changes are extraordinary measures for these institutions. But when facing a transformative threat and/or opportunity on the horizon, change measures may prove to be entirely prudent.

My sense is, though, that many more ARL libraries should be doing something about E-science than are yet doing so. Although it is still relatively early in the process of research library engagement in E-science, I fear that the time needed to prepare an organization for the type and scale of changes needed may be so great that already it is too late for those that have not yet started at least in a small way.

4.1. Small Changes

There are several examples of user-needs assessing by research libraries, using various qualitative methodologies to gain a better understanding of user behavior in order to design better systems and services. Two examples illustrate how results from these assessments can be interpreted as supporting changes that will more closely align research libraries with E-science activities. These examples correspond to market research and incremental change in Arms's framework.

In 2006 the University of Washington Libraries conducted an assessment of the information needs and uses of biosciences faculty members and graduate students (UWash 2007). The major themes that emerged from interviews and focus groups were the following:

- Google, PubMed, and Web of Science are the preferred starting points for all.
- More online journals, including older material, are wanted.
- Faculty and many graduate students go to the physical library only as a last resort.
- If material is not online they want digital delivery to their desktop.
- Discipline-specific branch libraries further splinter information-seeking and use.
- E-science is emerging as a new priority.
- Users lack awareness and understanding of many library services and resources.
- Interdisciplinary activity is increasing among sciences and across domains.

These findings were not a surprise to anyone. We could see the results of many of them playing out in our libraries. But the findings—expressed in the faculty and students' own words—have provided weight to the argument for change in library organizational structures, systems, and services.

A second study, by the University of Minnesota Libraries (UMinn 2007), also studied scientists' research behavior and information use, and resulted in findings quite similar to the Washington study. The Minnesota study made use of systematic ethnographic methods to analyze research behaviors and to construct a detailed framework of information processes and uses based on frequency. This provides a tool that can be used to determine how well-aligned library systems and services are to actual user needs and behavior. Among other findings, this study identified data curation as an emerging need and found that the university's libraries had little (in systems, staff, or services) to offer in this area. This finding suggested a need for further investigation into how to provide data curation.

These studies, and other similar works, provide evidence of the need for change and of the need to marshal resources necessary for making changes.

Several U.S. research libraries have begun to respond to the emerging E-science environment by forming groups of library staff members to raise awareness about relevant issues and to monitor developments. These groups are usually focused on data management issues and may explore opportunities in the local environment. These activities take little in the way of institutional commitment and require few resources to support. Such activities provide a low-cost way to develop expertise, monitor local conditions, and plan and coordinate a response as needed. Some data-issues planning groups have conducted data set inventories across academic departments and schools, and a few have conducted pilot data-management projects.

I can only speculate how many libraries have formed such internal data-issues planning groups. But I am confident that formation of such groups is the most widespread response to E-science to date among ARL libraries.

The University of Pennsylvania Library is a case in point. It convened a group of librarians to study and to discuss the ARL E-science task force report and begin to formulate a response. The group did background reading, met with faculty members who worked with data sets, and contacted library colleagues who were knowledgeable about E-science. One point emerging from the group's deliberations was the need to create persistent, unique identifiers for data sets, which could help users find data sets referenced in derivative publications (UPenn 2008).

Another development that fits here is the emergence from MIT's Earth System Initiative of esi@mit.edu, an e-mail list for a distributed, self-selected interest group. This list provides a forum for discussion of engineering and science data-management issues for anyone working with the rapidly growing volume of digital data coming out of the engineering and science research communities. Discussion topics include preliminary audits, pilot projects, planning for data management, the creation of standards and work flows, use of technologies, the social aspects of data sharing, and moving data into a system in which it can be preserved and reused. Science and engineering librarians at the Massachusetts Institute of Technology organized and manage this list. It debuted early in 2008 and has several dozen subscribers. This kind of communication mechanism, an example of self-initiated community organizing, can raise awareness and lead to the spread and adoption of model projects.

4.2. Medium Changes

Another indication of change in libraries, or perhaps preparation for change, is what librarians are meeting about. Recently, the Center for Library Initiatives of the Committee on Institutional Cooperation (CIC), a consortium of large universities in the Upper Midwest region of the United States, sponsored a two-day conference on librarians and E-science (CIC 2008). More than 100 staff members from CIC university libraries attended the conference. Scientists from various disciplines gave presentations on their research and on trends in data management. Librarians described their collaborations with E-science activities and projects, and federal government agency and national association representatives explained their perspectives. CIC librarians concluded the conference by developing a cooperative research agenda and identifying other specific activities on which they could commit to working.

I classify this as a medium-level change because, although it requires only a modest investment for any single institution—just the cost for a few staff members to attend a conference—it constitutes a significant commitment and investment for the consortium collectively. As such, it is a milestone. It indicates that a large segment of the U.S. research library community sees E-science as crucial to a vibrant future.

The Cornell University Library established a Data Working Group in 2006 to examine issues related to research-data curation, and to make recommendations for library engagement in this area. The group planned to present its recommendations in the form of a white paper to senior Cornell University library administrators, and its report was released in late 2008.

The Cornell working group has reviewed the ARL E-science report and is considering ways to participate in the resulting development of ARL resources and programs. One resource that the Cornell University Library may be interested in helping create is an inventory of discipline-based E-science centers and large-scale projects (Cornell 2008). Cornell's VIVO architecture and resource is a good example because it is a Web-based resource supporting collaborative work in the life sciences, bringing library and information resources together with profiles of life science researchers, including their research interests, publications, and courses taught (VIVO n.d.).

The University of Washington Libraries has taken a "medium change" approach, representing some commitment and investment, by creating a position for a staff member dedicated to investigating opportunities for the UW Libraries to be engaged with E-science activities on campus. (I held this exploratory, special assistant position from its creation in early 2007 until I took on other responsibilities in late 2008.)

The University of Washington Libraries also took the lead in developing a UW-based proposal in response to the NSF DataNet solicitation (see discussion in section five of this chapter). Just creating a structure and a process to develop the proposal proved to be a significant step in itself, particularly in terms of establishing relationships among people from disparate units and multiple disciplines. If the project receives a funding award, it will bring about huge change for the UW Libraries in response to E-science.

4.3. Big Changes (in Development)

Some large academic research libraries have been actively exploring roles for librarians in E-science for several years. Included are the libraries at Emory University, Johns Hopkins University, Purdue University, the University of California at San Diego, and the U.S. National Agricultural Library. The reader will find descriptions of those institutions' E-science activities in chapters one, three, seven, eight, and nine of this book. Another contributor of note to this developing body of work is the U.S. National Library of Medicine (NLM).

Overall, as Richard Luce has made clear elsewhere (Luce 2008), new organizational structures are needed to respond effectively to the E-science environment. In particular, Luce has posited the need for research libraries to transform themselves from a static discipline orientation to a team-based, multidisciplinary structure. He sees the need to form dynamic virtual teams that can respond to project needs at different phases: more intense staff dedication is needed at some points than at others. Departmental or subject liaisons may be well integrated with researchers but they are not usually able to respond dynamically to emerging trends with intense needs. Luce states:

> New organizational models should reflect the environments they are attempting to support, recognizing the synergy and interdependence between scholars and information pioneers. To proactively support this environment, librarians must become part of the research process, fully members of the research team. To do this, library staff members need to "go native" and embed themselves among the teams they support. Clearly this will have significant implications for the staffing profile and the workforce skill set. (Luce 2008)

As a transformational process—involving both organizational and work force dynamics—this is a work in progress.

5. Related Changes and Other Initiatives

5.1. Role and Future of Science Libraries/Librarians

We know with some confidence what the research needs and information uses are of the science, engineering, and health sciences researcher communities. Many studies have been conducted that shed light on this, although more granular research is needed to refine further the differences among disciplines. The University of Minnesota has published the most comprehensive bibliography of available studies that I have seen (UMinn 2005).

The emergence of E-science raises important questions about services and infrastructure within ARL libraries in support of science. Libraries may, in fact, be creating obstacles to emerging interdisciplinary models of science. Branch libraries based on separate collections in related areas of the sciences are cited as a hindrance to multidisciplinary research at a time when online access transcends discipline-based collections (UWash 2007). Other recent behavioral assessments suggest that libraries are often not perceived as part of the evolving research infrastructure in support of interdisciplinary, team science (UMinn 2007). There is a perception that science librarians, more than ever before, need to be integrated and actively engaged with their user communities. They need to understand not only the concepts of the domain, but also the research methodologies and norms of scholarly exchange. This level of understanding and engagement goes well beyond knowledge of the literature. It requires being a trusted member of the community with recognized authority in information-related matters. This new paradigm suggests a shift in focus from managing specialized collections (the branch library model) to one that emphasizes outreach and engagement. Many science librarians, of course, are already doing this. There are examples of science and health sciences librarians working with faculty in teaching courses, participating in research projects, and publishing. But research libraries need to consider how to extend these models and prioritize opportunities for engagement since there will not be enough staff or resources to cover all identified needs.

In the absence of systematic metrics to guide these decisions, many pilot projects may be the best we can do to develop experience and best practices, eventually leading to evaluation criteria that can support resource allocation decision-making. We need a community-wide effort to reconceive the science library for E-science (Luce 2008). Part of this effort needs to include a far-reaching consideration of what kind of library structure(s) and service delivery models will best meet the needs of various research groups. Determining this will be a challenge because one model will not fit all situations. Our existing structures and service models are clearly inadequate in the face of rapidly increasing interdisciplinarity and the proliferation of multi-institutional research teams (UWash 2007).

5.2. Other Initiatives Bringing Change in Research Libraries

5.2.1. U.S. NSF DataNet Federation

Potentially the single most significant driver of research library collaboration with E-science activities to date is the U.S. National Science Foundation (NSF) solicitation of partners for the Sustainable Digital Data Preservation and Access Network, known as DataNet (NSF 2007). The following is excerpted from the DataNet program description:

> one of the major challenges of this scientific generation: how to develop the new methods, management structures and technologies to manage the diversity, size, and complexity of current and future data sets and data streams. This solicitation addresses that challenge by creating a set of exemplar [sic] national and global data research infrastructure organizations (dubbed DataNet Partners) that provide unique opportunities to communities of researchers to advance science and/or engineering research and learning. The new types of organizations envisioned in this solicitation will integrate library and archival sciences, cyberinfrastructure, computer and information sciences, and domain science expertise

to . . . provide reliable digital preservation, access, integration, and analysis capabilities for science and/or engineering data over a decades-long timeline . . . and serve as component elements of an interoperable data preservation and access network.

By demonstrating feasibility, identifying best practices, establishing viable models for long term technical and economic sustainability, and incorporating frontier research, these exemplar organizations can serve as the basis for rational investment in digital preservation and access by diverse sectors of society at the local, regional, national, and international levels, paving the way for a robust and resilient, national and global digital data framework.

At the heart of the NSF DataNet vision is a new type of organization based on the research library as a model for stewardship, sustainability, and a focus on user needs.

Potential applicants should note that this program is not intended to support narrowly defined, discipline-specific repositories. This new type of organization is the research library transformed through a deep connection with and understanding of the needs and mores of the scientific research community, and through deep alliances with other entities involved in cyberinfrastructure.

Only five DataNet awards will be made. These five partners will form the envisioned DataNet Federation. This federation will form a web that will support a global digital data framework. Even though the "library" is the organizational model on which NSF is building the DataNet vision, there is no guarantee that all DataNet partners will feature research libraries in substantial roles, let alone give research libraries leading positions.

Even if the awardees feature ARL members or other research libraries in leading roles, these leaders will obviously be a small fraction of the library community. How, then, could this program be such a significant milestone in research library involvement in E-science? The program is significant because it establishes a model that will have a powerful influence on the wider community. It is a model that will impact many more institutions than those directly funded by NSF. This model has the potential to drive big changes in the research library community, catalyzing a transformation of the research library into one of the major players in the E-science arena.

5.2.2. U.S. NIH CTSA Initiative

Another U.S. federal agency effort deals with many of the same issues that are core to the DataNet development: the U.S. National Institutes of Health (NIH) Clinical and Translational Science Awards (CTSA) program seeks to transform the conduct of clinical and translational research in order to yield new treatments more efficiently and quickly. One of the ways to do this is through the design of new and improved clinical research informatics tools (NIH 2006).

The CTSA initiative, much like the DataNet Federation, seeks to develop a national consortium of institutions that will work together to transform how clinical and translational research is conducted. Much larger than the NSF DataNet program, the CTSA initiative includes twenty-four academic health centers at this point and is projected to grow to about sixty institutions within a few years.

There is much less of an explicit role for health sciences libraries in the CTSA projects that have been funded to date than for research libraries in the DataNet initiative. For one thing, development of a sustainable data network is not a stated goal of the CTSA program, so the library as a data steward is absent. However, several health sciences libraries are involved in CTSA projects at their institutions. Anecdotal evidence indicates that varying levels of collaboration are occurring in the design, development, and testing of informatics tools for data management. Several projects feature the development or refinement of ontologies and registries to enable interoperability among clinical data systems. For example, the Institute of Translational Health Sciences at the University of Washington (Seattle), a CTSA program, includes projects on access to electronic health data, clinical data management, access to scientific instrumentation data, and clinical data integration. These projects provide opportunities for librarians to collaborate with biomedical informatics researchers and clinical researchers.

5.2.3. Global Research Library 2020

Another development that bears watching for its potential to accelerate collaboration between research libraries and E-science activities is a series of workshops referred to as Global Research Library 2020 (GRL n.d.). There have been three gatherings so far—the first near Seattle in October 2007, the second near Perugia, Italy, in March 2008, and the third in Taiwan in February 2009. Microsoft Research has sponsored these gatherings, under the auspices of Tony Hey, corporate vice president for external research.

The focus of these workshops has been on how research libraries can support and collaborate with E-science researchers. The following is from the project description:

> The rapid dissemination of findings, the creation of new tools and platforms for information manipulation, and open access to research data have rendered the more traditional institution-based approaches to providing access to information inadequate. In order for research libraries to play a central role in this increasingly multi-institutional and cross-sector environment, we must find new approaches for how they operate and add value to research and discovery on a global basis. (GRL n.d.)

More workshops in this series are expected and products of great potential value to the research library community—e.g., a publication modeled after Towards 2020 Science (Emmott et al. 2006) and a research agenda—are planned.

5.2.4. U.S. National Library of Medicine

As mentioned in the introduction to this chapter, the decentralization of the U.S. research enterprise makes it extremely difficult to enforce or mandate policies that are closely tied to the progress of E-science—for example, policies on open access and open data. The examples discussed in this paper, therefore, are instances of single institutions responding to conditions as they see fit. At the level of the U.S. national libraries (Library of Congress, NLM, National Agricultural Library), there is relatively more possibility of having a concerted impact on the scientific communities served by them. The U.S. NLM is a noteworthy case in point.

The Entrez cross-database search system is a powerful federated search engine, or Web portal, that allows users to search many discrete health-sciences databases at the NCBI within the NLM, which is part of the U.S. NIH (Entrez n.d.). Entrez is an early, and still leading, example of an advanced search and analysis tool that allows researchers to search across multiple health-science databases, bringing together sources such as journal citations and abstracts, subject headings, full texts of journal articles and books, protein sequences, and gene sequence data. Entrez also provides an API enabling a structured interaction with all the databases and a flexible set of tools to discover unexpected patterns in the databases (Arms 2008).

There are many resources and tools developed by NCBI that have become critical elements in the progress of molecular biology and proteomics/genomics research (NCBI n.d.). One interesting example—linking disparate sources with potentially far-reaching ramifications—is the dbGaP database of genotype and phenotype. This database is designed to explore the association between specific genes and observable traits, such as the presence or absence of a disease or condition. Connecting phenotype and genotype data provides information about genes that may be involved in a disease process or condition, information that can be critical for better understanding the disease and for developing new diagnostic methods and treatments (dbGaP 2006).

These are powerful examples of products from the collaboration of domain scientists with computer and information scientists. With the knowledge and skills needed to use these E-science resources and tools, research librarians can support and connect with scientists in the scientists' own setting.

5.2.5. International Developments

There are many more international examples of E-science initiatives that involve libraries and librarians than I have space here to describe. Also, my knowledge of these efforts is limited. Those that I am aware of emerged from national (or multinational) initiatives and substantial federal government investment. Some also include partners and funding from other sectors. A few brief examples follow:

Canada: The Canadian Institutes of Health Research (CIHR) has adopted open access policies for publications resulting from CIHR-funded projects, and open data policies to ensure that data from research projects are available through appropriate public repositories immediately upon publication (CIHR n.d.). These actions have been taken in consultation with research librarians at the federal and provincial levels, and these policies have been implemented through deep partnering with the research library community (Bjornson 2008).

United Kingdom: For more than five years now, a wide-ranging E-science program has been built and supported by the research councils that fund arts and sciences research in the United Kingdom, the Joint Information Systems Committee, and other national partners. This coordinated effort has led to the development of systems, tools, and services that are becoming widely adopted in the conduct of research in the United Kingdom. The Digital Curation Centre is one of the products of this broad investment (RCUK n.d.).

European Union: DILIGENT (Digital Library Infrastructure on Grid Enabled Technology) is a prominent example of work being done in this area by the EU and its partners. DILIGENT brings together digital library and grid computing technologies. It enables scientists to collaborate on common research challenges through seamless access to all the resources they need, including content, applications, and computation. DILIGENT is a service-oriented application framework that provides for the building of transient virtual research environments (DILIGENT n.d.).

Australia: The Australian government has invested in several interrelated projects designed to support the management and life cycle of research assets, and to bring these resources and services to researchers across the federal and academic communities. The ARROW project has produced a robust repository for the publication of digital materials. ARCHER has created a collaborative research environment. Work may stay in ARCHER or migrate to ARROW as a published work through a "curation boundary"; that is, a work may evolve from an ephemeral to an archival object, and so move from one environment (ARCHER) to another (ARROW). The DART project, which relates to both ARROW and ARCHER, focuses on the issues around large data sets and sensors, as well as around annotation technologies and collaborative, composite documents (Treloar and Groenewegen 2007).

6. Conclusion

In 2006, Lougee, then chair of the ARL Joint Task Force on Library Support for E-Science, surveyed ARL directors for changes they were making in their libraries in response to the emerging E-science environment. The changes were few. Now, were we to repeat this informal survey of ARL members, we could be confident that there would be several more responses. The trajectory of change is in the right direction but the evidence cited in this paper indicates that we are still short of a critical mass. Awareness of the issues has been building within the ARL community since the ARL E-Science Task Force report was released. More discussions and meetings about the implications of E-science for research libraries are taking place.

A very few research libraries in the United States and Canada are in the process of making significant investments to transform their structures and services in a direction that supports E-science. A few more are making more modest changes to better position themselves to play a significant role in this arena. Many more are monitoring local, national, and global trends in this area and are internally assessing their strengths and options. I suspect that this will lead to more and bigger changes in the next one to two years. Within that time, it may prove useful to the research library community to repeat the snapshot I have attempted to provide through this paper, particularly if the new survey uses a methodology that would lead to a more detailed profile of the institutional environment, changes, and results.

The U.S. research library community lags behind many of its global partners in dealing with E-science due at least in part to the decentralization of the U.S. research enterprise and the lack of impetus and coordination that national (or more centralized) mandates provide. Individual institutions are to a greater extent on their own to invent their future in the absence of national or consortial initiatives. This may be changing with the passage of the NIH open-access policy into federal law and the growth of a related effort to promote the need for open data policies. These broad policy movements could have a profound effect on library roles. Equally profound will be the galvanizing effect of models that will emerge as a result of the NSF DataNet initiative and other efforts that lead to the creation of federations of libraries and research institutions committed to advancing E-science.

As Luce noted (in chapter one), to do this will require a transformation of research libraries through the creation of a powerful user-centric infrastructure that supports collaborative multidisciplinary science, putting data curation and support for virtual organization environments at the center of what libraries do.

7. References

NB: Internet addresses in the following references were accurate as of December 30, 2008.

ACLS. 2006. American Council of Learned Societies. Our Cultural Commonwealth: The Report of the American Council of Learned Societies Commission on Cyberinfrastructure for the Humanities and Social Sciences. http://www.acls.org/uploadedFiles/Publications/Programs/Our_Cultural_Commonwealth.pdf.

ARL. 2007. Association of Research Libraries. Joint Task Force on Library Support for E-Science. Agenda for Developing E-Science in Research Libraries. Final Report. http://www.arl.org/bm~doc/ARL_EScience_final.pdf.

Arms, W. Y. 2008. "Cyberscholarship: High Performance Computing Meets Digital Libraries." *Journal of Electronic Publishing* 11, no. 1 (Winter). http://hdl.handle.net/2027/spo.3336451.0011.103.

Bjornson. 2008. Personal communication to the author from Pam Bjornson, director general, Canada Institute for Scientific and Technical Information. May.

CIC. 2008. Center for Library Initiatives Conference on Librarians & E-science: Focusing towards 2020. Purdue University, May 12–13. Conference Web site: http://www.cic.uiuc.edu/programs/CenterForLibraryInitiatives/Archive/ConferencePresentation/Conference2008/home.shtml.

CIHR. n.d. Canadian Institutes of Health Research Web site: http://www.cihr-irsc.gc.ca/e/193.html. CIHR Web Page on Policy on Access to Research Outputs: http://www.cihr-irsc.gc.ca/e/32005.html.

Cornell. 2008. This information comes from a posting by Amy Stout, computer science librarian, Massachusetts Institute of Technology, on the esi@mit.edu e-mail list, April 3.

dbGaP. 2006. U.S. National Library of Medicine. NIH Launches dbGaP, a Database of Genome Wide Association Studies. Press release. December 12, 2006. http://www.nlm.nih.gov/news/press_releases/dbgap_launchPR06.html.

DILIGENT. n.d. About Diligent. http://www.diligentproject.org/content/view/73/257. Related information on the EU's Enabling Grids for E-sciencE (EGEE) project is at http://www.eu-egee.org/.

Emmott, S. J., E. Shapiro, S. Rison et al. 2006. Towards 2020 Science. Microsoft Research Cambridge (England). http://research.microsoft.com/en-us/um/cambridge/projects/towards2020science/downloads/t2020s_report.pdf.

Entrez, the Life Sciences Research Engine. n.d. Home page: http://www.ncbi.nlm.nih.gov/Entrez. A good description of Entrez is in Wikipedia: http://en.wikipedia.org/wiki/Entrez.

GRL. n.d. Global Research Library home page: http://www.lib.washington.edu/grl2020/index.html.

Hey, Tony, and Jessie Hey. 2006. "E-Science and Its Implications for the Library Community." *Library Hi Tech* 24, no. 4:515–28.

Luce, Richard E. 2008. *A New Value Equation Challenge: The Emergence of Eresearch and Roles for Research Libraries*. Washington, D.C.: Council on Library and Information Resources. Publication 142. http://www.clir.org/pubs/reports/pub142/luce.html.

NCBI. n.d. National Center for Biotechnical Information. Human Genome Resources page: http://www.ncbi.nlm.nih.gov/genome/guide/human/resources.shtml.

NIH. National Institutes of Health. 2006. National Center for Research Resources. Clinical Research Resources. Clinical and Translational Science Awards. http://www.ncrr.nih.gov/clinical_research_resources/clinical_and_translational_science_awards/.

NSF. 2007. National Science Foundation. Office of Cyberinfrastructure. Directorate for Computer & Information Science & Engineering. Program Solicitation: NSF 07-601. Sustainable Digital Data Preservation and Access Network Partners (DataNet). http://www.nsf.gov/pubs/2007/nsf07601/nsf07601.htm

RCUK. n.d. Research Councils UK. E-Science Core Programme Structure and Key Activities. http://www.rcuk.ac.uk/escience/coreprog/default.htm.

Treloar, Andrew, and David Groenewegen. 2007. ARROW, DART and ARCHER: A Quiver Full of Research Repository and Related Projects. *Ariadne*, no. 51 (April). http://www.ariadne.ac.uk/issue51/treloar-groenewegen/.

UMinn. 2005. University of Minnesota Libraries. A Multi-Dimensional Framework for Academic Support: Project Bibliography. http://www.lib.umn.edu/about/mellon/references.phtml.

UMinn. 2007. University of Minnesota Libraries. Final Report: Understanding Research Behaviors, Information Resources, and Service Needs of Scientists and Graduate Students: A Study by the University of Minnesota Libraries. http://www.lib.umn.edu/about/scieval/Sci%20Report%20Final.pdf.

UPenn. 2008. Excerpted from a posting by Amy Stout, computer science librarian, Massachusetts Institute of Technology, on the esi@mit.edu e-mail list, April 3. Related University of Pennsylvania resources are E-science readings at http://tags.library.upenn.edu/project/24973, E-science projects/centers at http://tags.library.upenn.edu/project/25018, and data citation at http://tags.library.upenn.edu/project/24988.

UWash. 2007. University of Washington Libraries. Biosciences Resources and Services Planning Task Force Final Report. http://www.lib.washington.edu/assessment/reports/BiosciencesFullFinal.pdf.

VIVO. n.d. Web site: http://vivo.library.cornell.edu/.

8. Appendix A

ARL Joint Task Force on Library Support for E-Science, 2006–2007

Members

Wendy Lougee, chair (University of Minnesota, USA)
Sayeed Choudhury (Johns Hopkins University, USA)
Anna Gold (Massachusetts Institute of Technology, USA)
Chuck Humphrey (University of Alberta, Canada)
Betsy Humphreys (National Library of Medicine/National Institutes of Health, USA)
Rick Luce (Emory University, USA)
Clifford Lynch (Coalition for Networked Information)
James Mullins (Purdue University, USA)
Sarah Pritchard (Northwestern University, USA)
Peter Young (National Agricultural Library, Department of Agriculture, USA)

ARL Staff Liaisons

Julia Blixrud (ARL, USA)
Neil Rambo (ARL/University of Washington, USA)

9. Appendix B

ARL Joint Task Force on Library Support for E-Science, 2006–2007
Recommendations and Strategies (Reproduced by Permission of ARL)

OUTCOME 1: An ongoing capacity and process within ARL to develop, coordinate, and evaluate an e-science program agenda.

STRATEGIES:

- Develop structure and processes for carrying out the ARL e-science program agenda, including a robust education and communication program.
- Coordinate and monitor progress on the outcomes, strategies, and action plans.

OUTCOME 2: A widely shared understanding both within research libraries and among other stakeholders in the e-science support community of how libraries can contribute to the development and ongoing evolution of cyberinfrastructure and e-science.

STRATEGIES:

- Build understanding at the level of library leadership of the potential for e-science to transform the process and conduct of research.
- Develop, in collaboration with other stakeholders and experts, a set of principles for research libraries' support of e-science.

- Articulate, both within ARL and with key education and research societies, a vision following from these principles and from existing models and exemplars, for research libraries roles in stewardship of research assets and as a consultant/partner in the full life cycle of scientific data.
- Build understanding at the practitioner level in the library profession of e-science support practices and needs.

OUTCOME 3: Knowledgeable and skilled research library professionals with capacity to contribute to e-science and to shape new roles and models of service.

STRATEGIES:

- Highlight exemplary programs and lessons learned.
- Identify gaps in library services and recommend steps that research libraries can take to address support needs of team science, including interinstitutional team science.
- Build a library workforce with relevant new skills and knowledge about emergent forms of documentation and research dissemination.

OUTCOME 4: Research libraries as active participants in the conceptualization and development of research infrastructure, including systems and services to support the processes of research and the full life cycle of research assets.

STRATEGIES:

- Actively monitor, understand, and engage in activity around emergent models in publishing, particularly publication with associated primary research data.
- Monitor developments in research tools and systems, e.g., electronic laboratory notebook systems.
- Monitor and document development of collaboration environments (e.g., through requests for proposals) to identify logical points in which research librarians and research libraries might play a role.
- Document development of discipline-based repositories.
- Support new forms of scientific data publication.
- Support long-term access to scientific data as part of the scientific record.

OUTCOME 5: Influence on policy, standards, and resource allocation decisions that support ARL principles.

STRATEGIES:

- Promote research library involvement in shaping policy and protocols with respect to emerging scholarly communication models that integrate data and publications.
- Develop mechanisms to be an active participant in the open data movement.

PART II

PERSPECTIVES FROM NATIONAL ORGANIZATIONS

Library and Information Technology Support of E-Science in the Western Context

Joan K. Lippincott

Introduction

In recent years, scientific instruments in space, in the oceans, on land, and in other environments have streamed massive amounts of data to scientists for their research. These very large data sets create unprecedented opportunities for research for the scientists who collected the data, and, if publicly available, the data sets also present opportunities for other scientists to use existing data for new purposes. However, with this abundance of data come many challenges. Scientists at Cornell University's Theory Center state that "scientific instruments that transform phenomena in the physical world into digital data and computer simulations of scientific experiments have created a data-driven revolution in the sciences. Scientists have moved from data-starved environments to conditions where research communities are overwhelmed with data."[1] There are opportunities and challenges for librarians and information technologists in university environments to support access to, management of, and preservation of these large data sets for research.

In the United Kingdom, the term *E-science* is used to describe the emergence of data-driven science. The United Kingdom uses a related term, *E-infrastructure*, for "the distributed computing infrastructure that provides shared access to large data collections, advanced ICT tools for data analysis, large-scale computing resources and high performance visualization. It embraces networks, grids, data centres and collaborative environments."[2] This is very similar to the concept of *cyberinfrastructure*, as described in a seminal report from the U.S. National Science Foundation

The author thanks Clifford Lynch, executive director, Coalition for Networked Information, for his review of and helpful comments on an earlier draft of this paper.

(NSF), which states, "The emerging vision is to use cyberinfrastructure to build more ubiquitous, comprehensive digital environments that become interactive and functionally complete for research communities in terms of people, data, information, tools, and instruments and that operate at unprecedented levels of computational, storage, and data transfer capacity."[3] Scientists working on projects using large data sets may use data generated by projects in other countries, and they may collaborate with other scientists in their own institutions and countries or in other countries. They utilize the high-performance data networks that have global reach and may use tools that reside in locations other than their home universities or research institutes. They may contribute to global or regional data sets in their individual disciplines, use data from other disciplines in new ways, or analyze a variety of data from different sources to develop visualizations or new kinds of analyses of important phenomena.

E-science or E-infrastructure and cyberinfrastructure are, by their nature, global in scope, yet regions of the world, countries, consortia of institutions, and individual institutions and organizations play active roles in building elements of cyberinfrastructure and in contributing to the body of knowledge within the framework of E-science. This chapter will provide an overview of E-science in selected areas of the West, particularly in relation to information technology and libraries, focusing on the advanced programs in the United Kingdom, with brief descriptions of developments in the European Union (EU) and Canada. Since other chapters in this volume will describe initiatives in the United States in E-science and cyberinfrastructure, this chapter will focus on initiatives of only one organization based in the United States—the Coalition for Networked Information (CNI)—and on its work to foster broader understanding of many issues and implications of E-science, particularly for librarians and information technologists.

The CNI is a joint program of an organization of major libraries in the United States and Canada—the Association of Research Libraries (ARL)—and EDUCAUSE, a nonprofit association whose mission is to advance higher education by promoting the intelligent use of information technology. CNI, ARL, and EDUCAUSE all have headquarters in the United States. CNI was founded in 1990 to support the transformative promise of networked information technology for the advancement of scholarly communication and the enrichment of intellectual productivity. It is an institutional membership organization, and its members come from a wide variety of sectors, including higher education, publishing, networking and telecommunications, information technology, government, foundations, museums, libraries, and library organizations. CNI works closely with many U.S.-based organizations including the Council on Library and Information Resources and the Digital Library Federation. While the majority of CNI's member institutions are based in the United States, the organization has members in Canada, Europe, and Australia. CNI has a long-standing collaborative relationship with the organization that manages networking and digital library programs for higher education institutions in the United Kingdom: the Joint Information Systems Committee (JISC).

Country and Regional Initiatives

Programmatic Focus and Initiatives in the United Kingdom

The government of the United Kingdom established an E-science program in 2001 and put into place a number of mechanisms to coordinate and fund the implementation of E-science initiatives. A primary role is played by the Research Councils in the United Kingdom (RCUK), of which there are currently seven in the fields of arts and humanities, biotechnology and biological sciences, engineering and physical sciences, economic and social research, medicine, natural environment, and science and technology facilities. These research councils, which predate the E-science program and have a broad mandate, were established by royal charter and are independent legal bodies outside of government but accountable to Parliament.[4] The UK E-science activity was initially led by Tony Hey, who subsequently became head of Microsoft Research, and his efforts and those of others resulted in early attention to this emerging area. Notably, the United Kingdom initiated its E-science program in 2001; the U.S. NSF did not publish its major planning document on cyberinfrastructure until 2003, and only in 2006 established an Office of Cyberinfrastructure.

As the initial five-year funding cycle of the UK's E-science program came to a close, a working group (Office of Science and Innovation e-Infrastructure Working Group) was formed to provide a guide to next steps. In February 2007, a major report was released on "Developing the UK's e-Infrastructure for Science and Innovation."[5] A steering group, comprised of representatives of the Research Councils, the JISC, the Research Information Network (RIN), and the British Library, wrote the document, which described the rationale for and the elements of a national E-infrastructure for research. The authors set their mission in the context of the need for the United Kingdom to realize its national economic objectives and its global responsibilities. The steering group set up working groups for six topical areas: (1) data and information creation, (2) preservation and curation, (3) search and navigation, (4) virtual research communities, (5) networks, compute [sic], and data storage, and (6) authentication, authorization, accounting, middleware, and digital rights management. The report provides details on findings and recommendations on these topics by area.

This steering group's report is remarkable on a number of levels. First, it brings together a number of professional communities—scientists, information technologists, librarians, and government workers—to forge a joint vision of the kind of infrastructure that will allow the United Kingdom to achieve its national research and economic aims. Typically, in other countries, each of these professional groups would issue its own report on directions for the future, and in fact, some of these groups, such as librarians, might be left out of the conversation altogether. As the report states in a section on cross-cutting themes, "The success of a UK e-infrastructure requires the development of a sense of joint ownership of that infrastructure and of a culture of sharing of research outputs. This depends on the active participation of a wide variety of disciplines, groups, and institutions."[6] Second, the report recognizes and indeed emphasizes the need for coordination at a number of other levels, including with industry in the United Kingdom and globally, and with international groups, especially in regard to technical standards. The report positions the E-science program as a vital resource for the economy, not as a separate "ivory tower" academic endeavor. Third, while recognizing the importance of the technology itself, the report strongly urges that issues related to the people involved, both researchers and those who support them (information technologists, librarians, and others) receive attention and resources. Specifically, all of the topical groups stressed the importance of training so that individuals and teams could take full advantage of resources developed in the E-science program.

Some of the recommendations of the report that have a particular relationship to libraries and technology support organizations include:

- the need for data standards, data integration and certification;
- funding for fundamental and applied research to address long-term digital preservation and curation needs;
- establishment of one or more national research data repositories as well as discipline-based data centers and services;
- development of search and navigation services, innovative tools, and training programs so that researchers can exploit them;
- finding aids for UK data;
- adoption of appropriate metadata standards;
- an investigation into how virtual research environments (VREs) can be linked with virtual learning environments;
- development of the capability to set up international research collaborations in virtual environments with minimal effort; and
- continued improvement of authentication and authorization services.[7]

The report and its recommendations are both concise and wide-ranging and provide a high-level blueprint for the future. More detailed reports of each topical group are available and linked from the main report.

The report's recommendations will influence the funding streams of many UK institutions, including the Research Councils and their partners. Many of the programs that emphasize the network, digital content, tools, and digital preservation are joint initiatives of the Research Councils and JISC, which is funded by the Higher Education Funding Council of England, the funding councils of Scotland and Wales, and some government education departments to provide direction and structure for information and communications technology (ICT) in support of higher and further education. The funding councils provide core support to the institutions of higher education in the United Kingdom, and the Research Councils provide grants for project support. JISC develops strategies for support of E-science and implements an "e-infrastructure programme" as one of its strategic initiatives. Some of the joint JISC/RCUK E-infrastructure initiatives are in these areas: operation of the high-speed network (SuperJANET 5), an integrated information environment, VREs, digital repositories, core middleware infrastructure and technology development, semantic grid and automatic computing, shared services, support for E-research, the Digital Curation Centre (DCC), the National Grid Service and Grid Operations Support Centre, and the National Centre for Text Mining.[8] This highly coordinated, centrally funded set of activities has no genuine counterpart in the United States.

In a document describing JISC's strategy for 2007–2009, the authors state, "The demands of the research community for e-infrastructure and data management have increased enormously over the past few years."[9] Therefore, JISC intends to increase its emphasis on E-science support and E-infrastructure in the near term. One step in this process is the development of a feasibility study for a UK research data center; an interim report on this initiative has been released.[10] Another step was a joint conference sponsored by JISC and the U.S. NSF that focused on cyberinfrastructure issues.[11]

While all of JISC's programs cannot be described within the constraints of this paper, one program will be singled out for its special interest to readers of this volume, namely the DCC. Created in 2004, the DCC was developed to "provide a national focus for research and development into curation issues and to promote expertise and good practice, both national and international, for the management of all research outputs in digital format."[12] The center is not a repository for large data sets; rather, it focuses on research, publicizes developments in data curation, disseminates information on standards, tools, and best practice, and provides services, software, and tools. The Research Councils support, often with partners, a set of data centers in the disciplines. The DCC provides expert advice to the community at large. Some of the current research initiatives that the center is pursuing include a security-oriented study on ensuring a safe data-analysis environment for astronomical data centers, standards and tools for the curation of scientific metadata produced at large-scale scientific facilities, and implementation of a pilot system to help create representation information for long-term data preservation.[13] The DCC held its third International Conference in conjunction with the Fall Task Force Meeting of the CNI in Washington, D.C., in December 2007, and held its next conference in Edinburgh, Scotland, in late 2008.

The center provides important support for a national policy that promotes the value of data for the overall progress of science and the economy. As a report on E-science curation states, "The UK's e-Science budget for 2001–2006 will total 213 million (GBP). Excellent digital curation is an opportunity to convert a proportion of these expenditures into capital in the form of an efficient, rich knowledge base, which itself supports and generates new science."[14] This view of the value of a generally available store of research data to the productivity of scientists, and the value of contributions to society made possible by such data, is echoed in an April 2007 report on data stewardship by the UK RIN. The report states,

> The essential goals we are seeking to achieve are thus to facilitate the advancement of research and innovation, to enhance the efficiency and effectiveness of research, and to

maximize the value of public and private investment in research. In pursuance of those goals, the fundamental policy objective is to ensure that: Ideas and knowledge derived from publicly-funded research should be made available and accessible for public use, interrogation, and scrutiny, as widely, rapidly and effectively as practicable.[15]

The report also proposes five principles:

1. roles and responsibilities of stakeholders such as researchers, research institutions, and funders should be clearly defined and they should create a framework of codes of practice,

2. digital data should be created and collected in accordance with international standards,

3. access to data should be provided in a way that maximizes ease of use and provides mechanisms for providing credit for data creators and protection of their rights,

4. the management and mechanisms for providing access to data must be efficient and cost-effective, and

5. data of long-term value should be preserved.[16]

Another national resource in the United Kingdom is the JISC-supported National Centre for Text Mining, which provides services and contributes to research.[17] In addition to language-related studies, this center supports text mining in such fields as systems biology and the study of proteins. The center collects biomedical corpora—selections of text from articles, databases, and other resources—to facilitate work in bioinformatics. The School of Computer Science at the University of Manchester leads the project and the Special Collections and Archives of the University of Liverpool Library provides expertise in information retrieval systems.

In the relatively brief period of the E-science program in the United Kingdom, great strides have been made. In a presentation at a JISC-sponsored E-science conference in 2006, David De Roure, a researcher from the University of Southampton, described the similarities and differences between the first five years of the VREs component of the JISC E-science program and the five years in the future. A VRE provides "a frame-work of resources to support the underlying processes of research."[18] The commonalities in the two VRE phases are that both support collaboration, large and small-scale research projects, and single and multidisciplinary research. However, the differences point out important progress in the development of these environments. De Roure envisions that VREs will move from being focused on technology to being focused on user and research practices, from being experimental to being developmental, from employing many different designs and approaches to employing a unified design and developmental approaches, and from adopting stand-alone solutions to adopting integrated solutions.[19] These distinctions reinforce the maturation of systems and the need for a unified environment that will enable users to benefit more easily from the resources being developed under the auspices of this program. While written to describe developments in a specific area, VREs, these changes can also be ascribed to the overall E-infrastructure in the United Kingdom.

The UK E-science program is notable for its policy-level statement of principles, its record of bringing together stakeholders, including scientists, information technologists, and librarians, to shape agendas jointly and develop priorities for national emphasis and funding, and its relatively quick development of significant projects that are carrying out research, development, and delivery of services to support E-science.

Programmatic Focus and Initiatives of the European Union

The EU's Sixth Framework program addresses needs of research and technological development that will involve and benefit more than one member country of the EU; this program is the main vehicle for funding research under EU auspices. The program identifies seven priority areas, including one of particular interest for E-science called "Information Society Technologies." In addition, there is a "New and Emerging Science and Technologies" field of research that complements the seven priority areas.[20] The EU program emphases in the "Information Society Technologies" area include communication, computing, and support technologies; knowledge technologies and digital content; and trust and security. Management of large data sets is not specified, but not excluded. Digital preservation is not specifically identified as a priority. However, other program priorities, such as "Aeronautics and Space," make specific mention of sensors and data information models. The "Life Sciences, Genomics, and Biotechnology for Health" area includes specific reference to bioinformatics developments.

The Sixth Framework seeks to create a European Research Area, which is "more than ever a cornerstone for a European knowledge society."[21] A 2006 paper from the EU identifies areas that need attention in order to overcome the fragmentation of research efforts and policies among EU countries. Of the six identified areas, three have a relationship to E-science, although that term is not used in the document. First, the report states that the EU should work toward building excellent research communities, including those that can work as virtual research communities. Second, the report states that world-class infrastructures, which need to be networked and integrated, should support research. Third, the report identifies "effective knowledge sharing" as a priority, including easy access to a public knowledge base.[22] The report also notes that some infrastructure projects include data repositories accessed via high-performance networks and grid technologies, and that cooperation among European countries and other regions outside of Europe will be needed to ensure the successful development and deployment of these repositories. In the section of the report describing issues related to sharing knowledge, the emphasis is on traditional modes of scientific communication such as databases of publications. However, the report also identifies some questions for examination, including whether there is a need for EU policies related to open access and dissemination of raw data as well as to outputs in peer-reviewed publications, when supported by public funds.[23]

The EU efforts place much emphasis on coordination of country policies and coordination of researchers within particular disciplines. There is less evidence of collaboration with the supporting infrastructures of libraries and computing, working as partners in these areas. A study on E-repositories has been commissioned by the

EU with the aim of identifying E-infrastructure requirements and presenting key issues. Some of the issues that will be considered have to do with technologies, standards, interoperability, sustainability, open access, and legal and economic concerns.[24]

Programmatic Focus and Initiatives in Canada

A report issued by the Canadian National Committee for the Committee on Data for Science and Technology (CNC/CODATA) provides a compendium of data activities in Canada as of 2006.[25] It illustrates the multi-layered, pervasive collection of large data sets in many scientific disciplines, including space sciences, atmospheric environment, biology, biotechnology, genomics, ecology, chemistry, climatology, crystallography, environment geomagnetics, geoscience, oceanography, and thermodynamics. Some collections are maintained separately under various types of administrative bodies, such as national science agencies. Some collections are maintained jointly by provincial government agencies, by disciplinary groups, or by collaborations with other countries such as the United States. The CNC/CODATA Committee reports to the director general of the Canada Institute for Scientific and Technical Information (CISTI). In the summer of 2008, CISTI announced the formation of a Research Data Strategy Working Group, chaired by the director general, and comprised of representation from universities, institutes, libraries, and funding agencies. The group will focus on identifying necessary steps to ensure that Canadian data is accessible and usable now and into the future.[26]

CANARIE, a longtime, worldwide leader in optical networks, which runs CAnet4, the high-performance network serving universities and research institutions in Canada, describes the evolution of the network in Canada. In four stages, the administrators of CANARIE have moved from the birth of a Canadian Internet backbone service to a pan-Canadian high-performance research and education network, then to a network with tools and applications that enable researchers to collaborate within Canada and with others around the world, and then to the current stage, which they designate "Lighting the Path to E-Science." In their 2006 annual report, they emphasize their role in supporting E-science projects by providing the capacity to send large quantities of data from sensors to research labs.[27]

E-science is clearly burgeoning in Canada, but the country's government is just beginning to organize cross-agency structures to promote a broad planning framework that includes scientists, information technologists, and librarians. The CISTI working group will address some aspects of data issues and include representatives from a number of sectors.

The Coalition for Networked Information and E-Science

In other chapters in this volume, the role of the U.S. federal government in E-science or cyberinfrastructure is delineated. However, in the United States, parties of more varied kinds play key roles in the development of research and technology initiatives. In particular, universities are significant players. Since many of the large

U.S. research universities are privately governed and other major universities are administered by state systems (and none is administered or primarily funded through a national government entity), the federal government plays a less direct role than in other Western countries in coordinating research initiatives and providing cohesive funding. While government agencies such as the NSF set agendas for their funding programs in cyberinfrastructure and other areas, organizations such as nonprofit associations also play an important role in identifying priorities, developing agendas, mobilizing universities, and disseminating information about new directions, best practices, and leading-edge initiatives. They may also have a role in lobbying the U.S. Congress for legislation to support and fund initiatives related to research.

Some nonprofit associations, such as the CNI's sponsoring associations, the ARL and EDUCAUSE, lobby on behalf of universities for funding for networking and library initiatives. They have committees that identify and address issues in a variety of areas; for example, ARL has a Library Support for E-Science Task Force, and the American Council of Learned Societies (ACLS) has a Cyberinfrastructure Report Task Force. The E-science task force has issued a report on library support for E-science.[28] EDUCAUSE has the Net@EDU program, of which the Campus Cyberinfrastructure Working Group is a part. Another major U.S.-based organization, Internet2, is an advanced networking consortium, providing high-end connectivity to its members. In addition, the National LambdaRail provides a high-performance optical network for portions of the U.S. higher-education and research community. Most associations sponsor meetings and workshops that promote agendas and provide information and training for new directions in the library and information technology professions. In 2006, the ARL sponsored a workshop on the long-term stewardship of large data sets under the sponsorship of the NSF. The workshop participants issued a report that identifies the challenges facing institutions that need to provide long-term access to rich resources of data. They also provided a set of recommendations for national funding and activities, which might be funded, in part, through the NSF.[29] CNI and ARL cosponsored in 2008 a forum on "Reinventing Science Librarianship" that included examination of the role that libraries are playing and could play in support of E-science.[30]

The CNI has three program themes and each has a relationship to E-science.[31] The themes are (1) developing and managing networked information content, (2) transforming organizations, professions, and individuals, and (3) building technology, standards, and infrastructure. CNI has a fourth programmatic area—policy and consultative activities—that includes the liaison activities of CNI's executive director with the U.S. NSF, the U.S. National Academies ("advisors to the nation on science, engineering, and medicine"), the Library of Congress, the National Library of Medicine, the ACLS, the JISC in the United Kingdom, and the United Kingdom's DCC. In the first theme, related to content, CNI seeks to promote deeper understanding of the institutional and disciplinary implications of E-research in the sciences, social sciences, and humanities. CNI cosponsored a workshop in late 2006 that focused on improving public access to publicly funded research. The content theme is also related to CNI's work in the area of institutional content repositories, which in the United States are seen as vehicles for providing long-term access to a variety of resources, including large data sets, rather than as storage and access mechanisms for eprints or preprints of journal articles, reflecting the more limited notion of institutional repositories prevalent in European countries. CNI wants to engage its community in a dialogue about institutional responsibility for a wide variety of information resources and assist with developing strategies for stewardship of these various resources.

In the second program area, related to organization, professions, and individuals, CNI seeks to assist institutions in understanding the kinds of staff that may be needed to provide stewardship of large data sets, and to identify exemplary institutions that can be used as models for others. In addition, CNI has held several Executive Roundtable meetings for administrators of university libraries and information technology activities to share perspectives on challenges of and potential solutions to organizational management issues related to large data sets. In recent years, CNI has hosted Executive Roundtables at its fall and spring membership meetings. At these roundtables, each of approximately 10 higher-education institutions sends a team consisting of its library director and chief information officer or similar individuals to discuss a preselected issue. In this way, some of the institutions that are doing leading-edge work in areas in which policies and best practices have not yet been developed can come together to discuss their institutional initiatives and learn from their colleagues at similar institutions. Executive Roundtable topics in recent years have included "Campus Infrastructure to Support Research: Managing Research Information and Data" (fall, 2005); "Institutional Cyberinfrastructure: Campus Planning and Strategies" (fall, 2006); and "Distributed IT, Information, and Informatics Services and the Implications for Central Organizations" (spring, 2007). The topics and concerns raised by participants in these roundtables included:

- models for determining what services regarding data stewardship should take place at the institutional level rather than at the global, regional, or country level;
- standards for metadata and data structures that would assist with interoperability;
- tools for providing access to data and facilitating the use of data in new ways;
- funding strategies for stewardship of large data sets, especially for long-term preservation and access;
- staffing models for data stewardship, as well as training and organizational placement of those responsible for data stewardship; and
- facilities (buildings) for housing server farms and facilities for provision of services.

Also in the facilities program area, CNI seeks to understand ways in which library and technology facilities can support and promote E-science initiatives in universities. In CNI's Learning Spaces program, examples are provided of innovative physical facilities that have been developed to assist scientists in doing collaborative work with the support of a digital infrastructure, and examples are provided of libraries that are showcasing visualization products of E-science on large screens in their information commons.

In the third program area, related to technology, standards, and infrastructure, CNI focuses on the more technical aspects of developing and managing institutional E-research or cyberinfrastructure. Some of the issues identified here include the implications and economics of storage of large data sets, requirements for long-term data management, curation, and preservation, and the need for informatics support services for faculty and researchers. In addition, the program addresses the needs of multiple campus collaborations, sometimes referred to as *collaboratories* or *virtual organizations*, and the technical infrastructure needed to support them.

In the early years of the twenty-first century, many in the information technology community in large research universities understood the notion of E-science and its implications for network infrastructure, development of distributed tools, and massive storage, but few academic librarians had even heard of the terminology of E-science or cyberinfrastructure. One of the key functions of CNI is to bring to the attention of our members to the critically important issues emerging in networked information. As early as the fall of 2002, Daniel Atkins, former director of the U.S. NSF's Office of Cyberinfrastructure, gave a talk at a semiannual CNI meeting where he presented the committee's preliminary findings and solicited comments from the meeting's participants.[32] Atkins served on CNI's Steering Committee for a number of years and helped the organization shape its perspectives and activities related to this important emerging area. Shortly after Atkins was named head of the U.S. NSF's Office of Cyberinfrastructure, he gave an update on the initiative at a plenary session at a CNI meeting in fall 2006.

In the summer of 2004, CNI announced to its membership that the ACLS had launched a Commission on Cyberinfrastructure in the Humanities and Social Sciences. CNI's Executive Director Clifford Lynch served as an advisor to the commission. An update on the project was presented at the fall 2005 CNI meeting along with a forum in which attendees were invited to provide comments to representatives of the committee.[33] In addition, numerous sessions have been held at CNI meetings in recent years on such topics as campus cyberinfrastructure, technical aspects of long-term data preservation, authentication and authorization, and text mining in the humanities.

CNI has played a number of roles in the cyberinfrastructure and E-science developments in the United States and in the United Kingdom. Through our programming at membership meetings, we alerted our constituencies about the importance of E-science and we assisted them in understanding some of the specific issues that affect library and information technology organizations within institutions, particularly research universities. We have connected some of the key leaders in cyberinfrastructure and E-science to strategic thinkers in the library and information technology professional communities so that they could share perspectives and form alliances. CNI Executive Director Clifford Lynch has provided valuable perspectives to the policy level initiatives on E-science and cyberinfrastructure in the United States and in the United Kingdom.

Conclusion

The support of E-science is an institutional, national, regional, and global challenge. Developing a high-level plan for the various relationships among key stakeholders, among the various geographic subdivisions, and among the disciplines involved is truly a major undertaking. An overall strategy would attempt to harmonize components and roles, and identify funding mechanisms. From the library and information technology perspective, a strategy should consider such important aspects as the robust nature of the network and the availability of tools for researchers, and should give attention to collections of data, interoperability issues, and preservation. Particular attention needs to be paid to governance, a process for decision-making, funding, and administration. E-science is still a relatively new area of research, but it is moving quickly. Infrastructures will be put in place to support specific projects without regard to interoperability or applicability to a broader framework unless institutions, countries, regions, and funders begin to put into place a policy framework that addresses needs for governance, funding, standards, administration, interoperability, and long-term preservation.

Librarians and information technologists can play more than a supporting role in E-science; they can assist with identification of key issues and can help set agendas to ensure progress that will have broad application in research activities. They can serve as valuable collaborators with scientists, government officials, and others. There is a need to understand what kinds of staff are required to run services, interface with scientists on issues such as kinds of tools needed, develop new kinds of metadata structures, build access interfaces, and develop innovative support services. In addition, there is a need to determine the kinds of physical facilities required to provide a home for these services. We will need large facilities for data storage, mechanisms for promoting E-science through teaching and learning, and awareness of this important new aspect of research.

Some countries such as the United Kingdom have made great strides in identifying and recognizing the important role that E-science will play in future research and have built governance, policy, and implementation frameworks that will facilitate achievement of national goals. The UK example is particularly notable for its consideration of library and information technology issues along with science issues as policy priorities, and its identification of directions. Library and information technology professionals can use the UK example as they work within their own structures to demonstrate the value and perspectives they can add to the conversation about E-science in their countries.

Notes

NB: Internet addresses in the following notes were accurate as of January 7, 2009.

1. Cornell University. Cornell Theory Center, "Data Driven Science," http://web.archive.org/web/20070525090953/http://www.tc.cornell.edu/Research/Data-Driven+Science.

2. "Developing the UK's e-Infrastructure for Science and Innovation." Report of the OSI e-Infrastructure Working Group, February 2007, 6, http://www.nesc.ac.uk/documents/OSI/report.pdf.

3. "Revolutionizing Science and Engineering through Cyberinfrastructure." Report of the NSF Blue Ribbon Advisory Panel on CyberInfrastructure, January 2003, ES2, http://www.nsf.gov/od/oci/reports/atkins.pdf.

4. Research Councils UK, "About Research Councils UK," http://www.rcuk.ac.uk/aboutrcuk/default.htm.

5. National e-Science Centre, "Developing the UK's e-Infrastructure for Science and Innovation." Report of the OSI e-Infrastructure Working Group, February 2007, http://www.nesc.ac.uk/documents/OSI/report.pdf.

6. Ibid., 12.

7. Ibid.

8. JISC, "e-Infrastructure Programme," http://www.jisc.ac.uk/whatwedo/programmes/programme_einfrastructure.aspx.

9. JISC, "JISC Strategy 2007–2009," http://www.jisc.ac.uk/strategy0709.

10. "UK Research Data Service Feasibility Study," UKREDS Interim Report, July 7, 2008, http://www.ukrds.ac.uk/.

11. "The Future of Scholarly Communication: Building the Infrastructure for Cyberscholarship," http://www.sis.pitt.edu/~repwkshop/NSF-JISC-report.pdf.

12. Digital Curation Centre, "Welcome," http://www.dcc.ac.uk/.

13. Digital Curation Centre, "Research & Development," http://www.dcc.ac.uk/research/#archiving.

14. Philip Lord and Alison Macdonald, "E-Science Curation Report. Data Curation for e-Science in the UK: An Audit to Establish Requirements for Future Curation and Provision." Prepared for the JISC Committee for the Support of Research (JCSR), 2003, 10, http://www.jisc.ac.uk/whatwedo/programmes/preservation/escience.aspx.

15. "Stewardship of Digital Research Data—Principles and Guidelines," http://www.rin.ac.uk/data-principles.

16. Ibid.

17. The National Centre for Text Mining, "Welcome to NaCTeM," http://www.nactem.ac.uk/.

18. JISC, "Virtual Research Environments Programme," http://www.jisc.ac.uk/whatwedo/programmes/programme_vre.aspx#VRE.

19. David De Roure, "E-Research the JISC Way" (talk with slides, UK e-Science All Hands Meeting, East Midlands Conference Centre, September 18–21, 2006), http://www.nesc.ac.uk/talks/ahm2006/keynote6.pdf. A video of the talk is at http://eprints.soton.ac.uk/41857/.

20. European Commission, "Sixth Framework Programme, 2002–2006," http://ec.europa.eu/research/fp6/pdf/fp6-in-brief_en.pdf.

21. Commission of the European Communities, "Green Paper. The European Research Area: New Perspectives," Brussels, April 2007, http://ec.europa.eu/research/era/consultation-era_en.html.

22. Ibid.

23. Ibid.

24. SCIDR, "Welcome to e-SciDR," http://www.e-scidr.eu.

25. Canadian National Committee for CODATA (CNC/CODATA), Report on Data Activities in Canada, 2006. September 2006, http://www.codata.org/canada/DAC/datact06_e.pdf.

26. Research Data Canada, http://data-donnees.gc.ca/.

27. CANARIE, CAnet4. Canada's Research and Education Network. "Annual Report, 2005–2006," http://www.canarie.ca/annualreport/areport_2006.pdf.

28. Association of Research Libraries. Joint Task Force on Library Support for E-Science, "Agenda for Developing E-Science in Research Libraries," November 2007, http://www.arl.org/bm~doc/ARL_EScience_final.pdf.

29. "To Stand the Test of Time. Long-term Stewardship of Digital Data Sets in Science and Engineering. A Report to the National Science Foundation from the ARL Workshop on New Collaborative Relationships: The Role of Academic Libraries in the Digital Data Universe," Arlington, VA, September 26–27, 2007, http://www.arl.org/bm~doc/digdatarpt.pdf.

30. "Reinventing Science Librarianship: Models for the Future" (Fall Forum sponsored by the Association of Research Libraries and the Coalition for Networked Information, Washington, D.C., October 16–17, 2008), http://www.arl.org/events/fallforum/forum08/index.shtml.

31. Coalition for Networked Information, CNI Program Plan 2008–2009, http://www.cni.org/program/.

32. http://www.cni.org/tfms/2002b.fall/abstracts/PB-NSF-Atkins.html.

33. http://www.cni.org/tfms/2005b.fall/project.html.

CHAPTER 6

HEAD IN THE CLOUDS AND BOOTS ON THE GROUND: SCIENCE, CYBERINFRASTRUCTURE, AND CLIR

Amy Friedlander

Probably one of Google's greatest achievements has been to make its name commonly synonymous with the term *to search* on the Internet and to make searching for information on the net an everyday occurrence. Yet it is only about 15 years, a single academic generation, since the advent of the net's widely accessible connectivity. Although the well-regarded Pew Internet and American Life Project reports that 73 percent of adult Americans are online,[1] that means that roughly one-fourth are not. Elsewhere in the world, robust Internet connectivity is not commonplace, particularly outside of Europe, Japan, Korea, and urban areas. In short, we are in the midst of a transformation in communication, and we have more to anticipate and imagine than to reflect upon. Our challenge at the Council on Library and Information Resources (CLIR) is to understand the convergence of these developments and to respond to them with leaders in higher education and research across all disciplines of the humanities, social sciences, and life and physical sciences, particularly as the developments affect the future of libraries, museums, archives, and other cultural and collecting institutions.

The transformations in scholarship are yoked to questions surrounding the role of the computationally intensive systems collectively known as the "cyberinfrastructure," which were created, engineered, and optimized over the last 30 years or so to support scientific research. Moreover, it is fairly clear that changes affecting libraries and sibling institutions are contextualized in a broad restructuring that consists of at least three related elements:

- a rethinking and reorganizing of the system of higher education in the United States over the next 30 years, including advanced research support, systems of scholarly communication, relationships with the private sector, and changes in the student population at the undergraduate and graduate levels;

- a rethinking of notions of literacy, how it is measured, and what it means to be literate;
- changes in the conduct of scientific research.

Concerning the latter, scientists have shared their results and interpretations for millennia, if we think of Aristotle and his students in the context of an oral tradition of scientific communication. Professional journals have enabled the written communication of scientific results, but in the last 30 years, collaborations have begun to occur earlier in the research process so that data as well as results are communicated and shared. This phenomenon is particularly obvious in large-scale scientific experiments and in the construction of shared databases, such as the Protein Data Bank. Moreover, we are also seeing the rise of the so-called citizen scientist, particularly in integrative sciences such as ecology that have enormous needs for computer processing or for broadly distributed, highly detailed observations that would be prohibitively expensive to obtain without volunteers.

Within these concurrent, seismic processes lies a set of interactions and feedbacks with advances in information technology, making the information technology, in its many expressions, both cause and effect. In this context, it is useful to think of the information technologies as creators of a computationally rich environment with a set of properties and affordances rather than as a specific set of technologies (for example, networking or word processing programs) or toolkits (for example, geospatial, statistical, or text analysis packages). Finally, making generalizations about a subject as large and heterodox as scientific research is always a perilous business. Much of what follows about scientific research might be said of research generally. Moreover, my comments are U.S. centered—because my professional experience has been almost exclusively in or about the United States. Almost certainly many counter-examples and nuances could be introduced to qualify some rather broad assertions. But let us go forward nonetheless, recognizing that these remarks are analogous to a view of earth from the moon.

Cyberinfrastructure and Science

The term *cyberinfrastructure* originated in a report by the U.S. National Science Foundation (NSF), which defined it as the comprehensive infrastructure required to capitalize on advances in information technology; cyberinfrastructure "integrates hardware for computing, data and networks, digitally-enabled sensors, observatories and experimental facilities, and an interoperable suite of software and middleware services and tools."[2] The American Council of Learned Societies subsequently adopted the term in its report on a cyberinfrastructure for the humanities,[3] and the word has crept into routine discourse in higher education and advanced research. Historically, roots of this idea extend back to the development of computer networking in the 1960s and advances in high-performance computing in the 1980s that enabled distributed research teams and electronic access to data and other resources. These developments made possible computationally intensive analyses in a range of fields, from computer-assisted design in engineering and manufacturing to spectroscopy and the construction of massive databases of highly granular information in the life sciences, social sciences, and physical sciences.

In parallel, the term *E-science* originated to name a broad research initiative that was formally organized in 2001 in the United Kingdom.[4] E-science has come to mean computationally intensive research that is executed in distributed network environments or involves large quantities of digital data and is frequently conducted by research teams.[5] Thus E-science and cyberinfrastructure, while closely allied, actually represent slightly different emphases. E-science connotes a research program; cyberinfrastructure recognizes the role that the engineered and institutional infrastructure plays in instantiating and fostering computationally-intensive research and, importantly, devotes resources to advancing the capabilities of the infrastructure. This is an important distinction, and one that helps us understand the roles of libraries, archives, and museums in supporting and nurturing the research enterprise.

The progress in the sciences toward a shared infrastructure is fairly well understood, at least in its broad form. There are several drivers: One is simply the cost of instrumentation and the limitations to broad distribution of these expensive facilities. Supercolliders, telescopes, sensor arrays, and so on are expensive to build, limiting the number that can be reasonably supported. There used to be fewer constraints on the number of suitable sites for such facilities. For example, Vassar College built an astronomical observatory in the nineteenth century for pioneering woman astronomer Maria Mitchell on its campus in Poughkeepsie, New York, only 75 miles north of New York City in the Hudson River Valley. Now, prime observing sites for modern observatories have fairly stringent requirements, and there are just a relative handful in places such as Hawaii, Chile, and northern Japan. Satellite-based earth-observing systems have similar constraints, such as where good downlinks can be located, and how monitoring and observations can be coordinated on a 24/7, global basis. Dealing with such constraints requires international collaborations across several facilities.

Cost and geography are two fundamental constraints. Speed of light is a third. Complex manipulation and rendering of very large data sets require the capabilities of a supercomputer or cluster. Moreover, while the network does enable computational tasks to be distributed, some problems result in collocation of resources, and some kinds of problems cannot be parsed into subtasks that can be cleanly distributed. Increasingly, there is discussion about different configurations of high-capacity computational resources and facilities: grid computing, cloud computing, supercomputer centers with high-speed lines affording access to a distributed but typically limited community of investigators. These four fundamentals—cost, geographic and environmental requirements, speed of light, and character of the research problem—together with advances in networking set up a tension between centralization and distribution evident in large-scale system architectures and in the social organization of the conduct of the research.

Finally, as Christopher Greer, former director of the National Coordination Office for Networking and Information Technology Research and Development, said at a forum organized by the Association of Research Libraries (ARL) on science librarianship, in mid-October 2008, the very "pillars of science" have changed, and modern scientists in many fields expect access to data and computational facilities to form the environment in which they will conduct their work, melding theory and experiment as well as legacy data, observations, analysis, and simulation in their intellectual quests.[6] Thus the E-science (or the research program) acts and is acted upon by the cyberinfrastructure, and the cyberinfrastructure has been evolved and will continue to be evolved to enable the E-science. And the systems will be both centralized and distributed.

On the one hand, the rise of so-called big science is obvious both in the scale of the instrumentation, such as the Large Hadron Collider at the European Organization for Nuclear Research (CERN) or the Stanford Linear Accelerator outside of Palo Alto, California, and in the organization of large research teams. On the other hand, networked access to resources, in particular to standardized data in digital form, has allowed for distributed research. In 1997, the State of São Paulo Research Foundation in Brazil (FAPESP) established a network of 30 research laboratories to form a virtual institute devoted to genomic projects, beginning with examination of pathogens in plants of local economic significance, notably citrus fruits and sugar cane. The research agenda subsequently expanded to include livestock and human cancer genomic research, and the network for ONSA (a program for human gene discovery) now comprises more than 60 participating institutions, including international partnerships.[7]

These two examples—CERN and FAPESP—put faces on such phrases as "globalization" or "internationalization" of the conduct of science. As of the end of 2006, CERN counted 11,046 paid and unpaid employees, researchers, and users drawn from more than 20 counties, organized into 13 onsite departments or units.[8] The six experiments at CERN engage international teams that range in size from 1,700 scientists from 159 institutes in 37 countries on the ATLAS experiment to 22 scientists from 10 institutes in four countries on the Large Hadron Collider forward experiment.[9] The researchers may not be physically present at CERN all of the time, but they do depend upon the experiments that take place at the facility. FAPESP, on the other hand, is a distributed social and organizational system of bench science. Large-scale coordination is enabled by the physical network, by consensus within the professional community on the structure of the data (the proteins, genomes, and so on), and by access to core data sets around which the conduct of the science has become organized. Access to such data sets are critical to observational sciences, like biology, ecology, climate studies, and so on, where the research relies heavily on highly granular data and may benefit from collections created on multiple geographical scales. Consistency in the way that those observations are captured, stored, and made available enables the entire community of researchers to contribute to and reuse the shared resource. Thus the infrastructure to support research is both centralized and distributed, and is both physical, in terms of lines, nodes, equipment, and so on, and informational, encompassing both the logical layer that integrates the disparate hardware and the conceptual structure of the biological data itself. The latter allows simultaneous storage, access, distribution, and analysis by diverse researchers who share a single set of databases.[10]

Earlier engineered infrastructures tended to be conceptualized primarily in terms of their physical representations as roads or telephone lines with their associated organizational and informational control systems. Moreover, there is a relatively clean distinction between operation of the infrastructure and services that were built because the infrastructure existed. An obvious example in the U.S. context was the collocation of stockyards, grain elevators, and flour mills with railroad junctions and canal facilities. In contrast, the cyberinfrastructure includes a data layer as an integral component.[11] Now, what we mean by "data" and the ways in which data will be managed remains an important discussion. But when data that is independent of the control systems required to manage the engineered network become part of the infrastructure, then information-managing entities, such as libraries, archives, museums, and corporate data centers, assume a larger and more explicit role in the infrastructure itself. Rather than being services and resources collocated with the infrastructure, entities such as libraries, archives, and data centers become integral to the operation of the infrastructure as users experience it and expect to use it. Perhaps not all of these agencies' traditional functions will migrate to the infrastructure, but some subset of them will, thus begging more questions: Which services are infrastructure services? Which ones are not? And are all libraries and collecting institutions equally vital to the success of the research enterprise?

Implications for Libraries

Arguably, libraries, archives, museums, professional societies, and related organizations have always been part of the organizational infrastructure that has supported research and education, articulating practices, standards, and codes of conduct that knit together various components. Interlibrary loan, MARC records, catalogs and abstracts of manuscripts, professional certifications, finding aids, indexes, and ISO standards all speak to codified practices that are intrinsic to modern research. More generally, librarians, archivists, and scholars have reached broad consensus on the functions associated with such institutions: They collect, preserve, and manage information made available to patrons under conditions that range from completely open to highly restricted, based on the nature of the material, community expectations, and local mores.

Conceptually, infrastructure systems are both hierarchical and scalable so that they meet local conditions but possess overall coherence and interoperate to obtain ubiquity, shareability, and broad access. Libraries and their various counterparts embody precisely this set of characteristics: They exist in many languages, meet a range of local or specialized needs, and manage a welter of information artifacts, yet they have formal and informal mechanisms for interacting and exchanging information and training across institutional, geographic, and political boundaries. In short, you can probably go into almost any library in the world and recognize that you are in one even though you also quickly understand that there are differences among them. And as my examples of CERN and FAPESP imply for research generally, libraries that support education and research are having to learn when to consolidate and centralize, when to distribute tasks, and how to maintain large-scale coherence at multiple scales, whether within the home college or university or as part of much larger systems. We can see evidence of this tension already in the intense discussions taking place about journal archiving, retention of physical copies, and access to licensed material. In the future, such traditional measures as gate count and physical collection size may become less useful as ways to gauge impact than metrics that capture intangible usage.

The introduction of digital technologies has greatly amplified this tension between the local and the system-wide. The cumulative effect of three developments—more power at the desktop, access to high-bandwidth networks linking researchers to each other and to other resources, and the existence of key resources such as scientific data sets and electronic journals—has been to push functions hitherto associated with the library toward the end user, and to increase demands on the library's stewardship and long-term data-management responsibilities. Students and faculty arrive on campus with fairly high expectations about the extent to which devices and programs will be supported, and campus administrators face hard choices about what to support as part of the campus infrastructure.[12] Although the library is much loved and greatly respected, it has receded from view. Surveys of U.S. faculty and librarians commissioned by Ithaka in 2006 found that "in the future, faculty expect to be less dependent on the library and increasingly dependent on electronic materials."[13] Just as technology has decoupled content from its artifactual form (typically the codex), so too has information from the perspective of these users become separated from the organizations that make it available—the publishers, aggregators, libraries, and so on—even while seemingly "free" access to a journal may be financed by a site license that the library or the university has negotiated.

My point is not to argue open versus restricted access but rather to show that the logic of the technology has been to push functionality to the desktop and to curtain off from that desktop a maze of systems and decisions. Indeed, recent developments in Web 2.0 services, cloud computing, application programming interfaces (APIs), and increased mobility have pushed some capabilities back onto shared services to which powerful yet lightweight devices will presumably have reliable and secure access. Therein lies a paradox: The empowered user is, in fact, enmeshed in and dependent upon an interlaced technical and organizational environment. And the operation of that environment—like the operation of the library—is essential yet unseen.

So what do libraries and other collecting institutions do? Certainly they provide integrative functions and they become, more than ever, stewards of collected knowledge. The same survey that found little support among faculty for librarians as gatekeepers also found widespread support for the library's preservation function. The importance of data curation, archiving, and preservation functions to the research library was a recurrent theme in a conference at CLIR, in late February 2008, on the future of the research library in the twenty-first century.[14] And the solicitation for "Sustainable Digital Data Preservation and Access Network Partners" by the Office of Cyberinfrastructure at the U.S. NSF placed substantial importance on the contributions of library and archival science. The solicitation called for organizations that "integrate library and archival sciences, cyberinfrastructure, computer and information sciences, and domain science expertise" to provide reliable and long-term data management, meet user needs and expectations, support research, and serve as components in an interoperable network of data preservation and access.[15] Ominous predictions of a data deluge within the scientific community are almost commonplace, and reports from the market intelligence firm IDC on the growth of digital information, primarily from the standpoint of the data storage community, echo and amplify these statements. A 2008 study reported a compound annual growth rate of information between 2001 and 2006 of about 60 percent and an excess of data over storage capacity in 2007, as predicted in an earlier report. Together with more regulatory requirements for information retention in the commercial sector, these developments, the authors concluded, put "greater pressure on those responsible for storing, retaining, and purging information on a regular basis."[16]

"Storing, retaining, and purging" sound a lot like appraisal, selection, acquisition, and weeding—functions well known to librarians and archivists. While perhaps the visibility of the reference function may be diminishing (and I am not entirely sure that it is), the collection management functions, including curation, preservation, and archiving, are increasing substantially in volume and difficulty. The information is highly heterogeneous, combining analog formats with a range of digital formats, standards, and platforms. The technical issues of preservation are well known: obsolescence of hardware and software, including operating systems, applications, and storage and access devices; error identification and management; intellectual property requirements; and data confidentiality and security. Users, however, expect data to be accessible and interoperable, and distinctions between "data" and "information" or "books" and "manuscripts" or "primary" and "secondary" sources, not to mention "libraries" and "archives," seem to melt away. But not entirely.

Different regulatory and access regimes are still tied to such distinctions, and although revisions to the copyright statute in the United States are slowly lurching forward, terms like "books" and "manuscripts" do not simply denote an arbitrary container for sequences of bits. They convey tangible and intangible information, meaningful to researchers, that applies to the use of the objects and the trust they instill. A biography of Jane Austen is simply not equivalent to her letters even if both are rendered in digital form, and a publication in a peer-reviewed journal carries weight independent of the preprint or conference paper that might have become available six months earlier. More problematic are new kinds of objects such as Web sites that are intentionally dynamic or may not be wholly self-contained, posing challenges for the librarian or archivist who seeks to enable users 10 or 15 years hence to re-experience objects as authors intended and to understand the various social and technical contexts in which to employ or interpret them. Finally, data, unlike publications, frequently carry restrictions to protect personally identifiable information or information, such as the locations of archaeological sites or mineral resources, that is deemed sensitive and therefore considered confidential. Anecdotal information suggests that some scientists, moreover, whose publications may rest on unique access to their hard-won data, have often proved reluctant to release that data to more general use. Or they may simply be unaware of the data's potential long-term value. Thus, notions of reusing and repurposing data are not widespread in scientific research, and the value of preservation (not to mention the ease with which it might be accomplished from the desktop) may be admired in the abstract but not considered necessarily relevant to an investigator.

Not surprisingly, then, building digital collections for the future requires attention to discovery and access, and active management of digital archives is more than keeping track of formats, platforms, and machines. In particular, requirements for interoperability have both technical aspects and implications for discovery and use. Especially among social and behavioral scientists, it is unlikely that designers of individual systems will know ahead of time all the kinds of information that an investigator might wish to assemble and analyze with a single set of tools. Research in epidemiology, which may engage data from the cellular to the societal as well as studies of climate change, public health, the environment, and ecology, is an obvious example of an integrative domain (or systems science) in which highly heterogeneous information, ranging from sixteenth-century travelers' accounts to twenty-first-century sensor measurements, might be relevant. Although librarians might not be researchers' gatekeepers, they are likely to be well positioned as recommenders, helping researchers to understand the range of information, how to get to it, and how to use it. They would use a blend of skills formerly associated with cataloging, reference, and subject specialties so that the information is seamlessly there for the end user, who does not need to know all the magic taking place behind the curtain.

CLIR's Role

CLIR is the successor organization to two older entities: the Council on Library Resources, formed in 1956, and the Commission on Preservation and Access, organized in 1986. CLIR itself was created in 1997 and inherited from both parent organizations a commitment to the preservation, access, stability, and management of research library collections. Since the appointment of Charles Henry as president in 2007, CLIR's programmatic agenda has been organized into six major related and mutually reinforcing topics:

1. Cyberinfrastructure: What are the technical and organizational systems, services, and relationships required to support an extensible, scalable network of data and services?
2. Preservation: What is required to manage data for effective use over the long term?
3. Digital scholarship: How does the new environment allow us to ask new questions not otherwise possible to answer?
4. Emerging library: What will the role of the library be in the future?
5. Leadership: How do we prepare students for a future in libraries and information work, and what will a career path look like over the course of a professional lifetime?
6. New models: What kinds of organizations and frameworks should we build in the United States and abroad?

In addition, in pursuit of a coordinative role in the developing cyberinfrastructure to support higher education and advanced research, CLIR seeks formal and informal partnerships and collaborations with other entities. Major efforts have been directed toward working with federal agencies, notably the Institute of Museum and Library Services, the NSF, the National Endowment for the Humanities, and the Library of Congress. Successful collaborations have been achieved by contributing to and participating in programs of these agencies, or by obtaining awards for funding from their grant programs, or by creating joint projects. CLIR also seeks to help graduate students when possible by articulating well-defined tasks that can be handed off to them, thus providing them with support, integrating them into CLIR's program and hence into information professions, and building partnerships with leading schools of library and information science. Such arrangements have been put in place with the University of North Carolina at Chapel Hill and the University of California at Los Angeles. These informal efforts amplify our formal programs directed toward library students, doctoral research candidates in the humanities, postdoctoral interns, and future library leaders.

Historically, CLIR's interests have resided more in the humanities than in the sciences and social sciences. In 2008, however, we increased our participation in programs that emanate from the scientific research agencies. Our participation takes two principal forms: participating directly in the research agenda, particularly when decisions concerning data management draw on library and archiving expertise; and convening activities across agencies and disciplines when there is common cause to be found among a broad range of researchers. Not surprisingly, these are both complementary avenues into a matrix of related issues involving digital scholarship, preservation, and cyberinfrastructure, which are three of our program areas. The very fact that it is so difficult to separate the strands speaks to the tight integration of the substance of the scholarship with the data, services, and systems on which that scholarship is predicated. That is why these topics interest us and why we believe that the roles of libraries, archives, and other stewardship institutions are simultaneously intuited to be important yet remain difficult to parse. That ambiguity is likely to remain with us for some time to come, precisely because the larger context of scholarship and higher education is, itself, unsettled.

With respect to the first dimension of our work with the basic science research agencies, the flagship effort is probably our support for the Blue Ribbon Task Force on Sustainable Digital Preservation and Access, sponsored by the NSF, the UK Joint Information Systems Committee, the Library of Congress, and others, including CLIR. By now, it is fairly well understood that more data is created by computationally intensive science than can be easily managed, and that over the long term, management of that data cannot be borne by the research agencies.

In addition, valuable data are created outside of the scope of traditional research by entities that have no apparent motive for the long-term preservation of this material. For example, economists and sociologists who are studying information-technology deployment in general have trouble finding suitably detailed information to complement the aggregate data compiled by the U.S. federal statistical agencies, which also tend to be very conservative in their sampling and analytical methodologies. The limitation in access to data affects certain microeconomic studies of firms, salaries and wages, and pricing. One solution is to use private sources of information, but these are expensive and can be limited by issues of confidentiality and proprietorship. Leading scholars have employed data supplied by the business intelligence and marketing company Harte-Hanks. But not only are the data sets expensive; they also naturally reflect the interests of the company's clients who have paid for the initial surveys. The content of the data files is geared toward marketing and not necessarily toward answering questions that investigators may have, and there is no guarantee that the data will be preserved, a problem that constrains long-term longitudinal comparisons as well as the ability of later scholars to validate earlier results by reexamining the data.[17]

This is a huge problem. Validating prior results, whether it takes the form of rerunning the experiment or checking the sources, is central to scholarship across the disciplines and goes to the heart of the trust model that supports advanced research. Thus data preservation is integral to computationally intensive research, whether in the sciences or the humanities, and libraries, archives, and museums, as stewards of data, are lynchpins in the infrastructure that supports and enables the conduct of research and the managing of its products in whatever form those products take. The realities may be somewhat harsh: data-management needs outstrip the capacity of the basic research agencies to pay for it indefinitely; important data lie outside the scope of the federal agencies; and owners of the data may have no obvious interest in sustaining the data indefinitely or in providing access to it.

The task force does not propose to address all of these issues, but it does propose to set the conceptual framework within which we can come to terms with the basics, namely, how much does it cost and who should pay? Among the early conclusions is a recognition, reached also by a project in the United Kingdom called LIFE (Life Cycle Information for E-Literature), that there will be a life cycle in the curation of information as the various interests of owners and custodians of data evolve. Data may be initially preserved to comply with regulatory requirements, such as the Sarbanes-Oxley Act, which governs financial and accounting information held by institutions subject to federal regulation. But when the period mandated by Sarbanes-Oxley expires, the information still might have historical value and hence public interest, which might lead to a transfer of custody of the material with necessary safeguards to protect confidential and proprietary data.

Under CLIR's role of convening symposia and workshops to identify common research challenges are two events. The first, a workshop, took place in late November 2007 and addressed what Gregory Crane of Tufts University called the "million books" problem.[18] When text corpora become very large, in some measure as a result of mass digitization projects, only the computer can "read" the text. The need to work effectively with these collections begins to push computer science research in the areas of multilingual services (embracing both information retrieval and machine translation), semantic disambiguation (in multiple contexts ranging from individual and place recognition to more abstract meaning), and document structure. Thus, we begin to see how a common agenda arising from the convergent interests of humanists and computer scientists is possible with the active engagement of librarians and archivists who are responsible for management and long-term viability of the data.

CLIR continued to examine the shape and form of this convergent agenda in a second workshop cosponsored with the National Endowment of the Humanities, which took place on September 15, 2008. (A formal publication was scheduled for early 2009.) Again, the domains represented were those traditionally associated with the humanities, such as history, art history, and literature, but the research challenges applied as much to the computer scientists as to the humanists, and as one social scientist told me, these questions could be asked equally well of his community. The goals of the one-day workshop were two-fold:

- to explore how advanced technologies enable new, deeper, and richer analysis and inter-pretation of text, video, sound, and other forms of creative expression traditionally grouped under the rubric of the humanities, and to understand the resulting implications for research on information technologies; and

- on the basis of that discussion, to formulate questions and topics that may represent the convergence of research issues and are distinct to the digital environment.

Underlying these goals is the acknowledgement that technology development is not a linear process of basic research, technology transfer, applications, and deployment. Rather, the application layer itself is iterative and dynamic, and research entails engagement and reengagement with diverse user communities, especially user communities that pose hard problems. Moreover, as the information universe expands, many of the research techniques associated with the humanities will flow over into the sciences as investigators navigate the millions of pages in preprint archives, journals, lab notes, and so on.

Finally, in March 2008, The Andrew Mellon Foundation awarded CLIR a significant grant to support a competition for cataloging so-called hidden collections. This generous grant addresses a problem that the research library community has studied for about a decade, namely, the existence of unprocessed, uncataloged, and essentially undiscoverable yet tremendously valuable materials held in the special collections of libraries, archives, museums, and historical societies. Estimates of the sizes of these hidden collections vary from 15 percent of the printed volumes in university special collections to an average of 27 percent of manuscripts, 35 percent of videos, and 37 percent of audio materials, according to surveys conducted by the ARL.[19] The goal of CLIR's program is to create, over five years, a distributed, multi-institutional Web-accessible catalog to materials of scholarly value that are currently inaccessible except to those specialists who may stumble across them in the course of their research or who may be directed to them by skilled librarians and archivists.

The grant is for one year with four one-year renewal options, based on our performance in the first year. We opened the competition in the early summer and expected to make the first award by the end of 2008. Right now, eligible collections must be owned or held in the United States, but in future years, we hope to expand the scope to include international participants. We are completely open on format, technical platform, and schema, requiring, however, that the resulting records be findable by future search engines and hence compliant with existing standards and protocols. Primary weight will be given to the research merit of the collections and then to innovations in cataloging and description that will enable increased discovery and access. Finally, CLIR will not hold the cataloged records in a centralized repository, although it is possible that a third-party aggregator may assume that responsibility. Rather, we insist that the organizations that own the materials must also accept responsibility for making catalog records and sustaining a Web-accessible catalog containing them, although, again, there are many ways to achieve such sustainability, including working with an aggregator or a third-party service.

We view this project as both a research experiment and an element in the evolution of the cyberinfrastructure to support research. The reasons are clear: We expect to learn a lot about efficient cataloging of rare materials, which has long been a time-consuming and labor-intensive process. We will probably learn more about how organizations build cyberinfrastructure through cooperation and resource sharing while minimizing the free-rider problem that has historically plagued centralized construction and delivery of infrastructure systems. Finally, the purpose of research infrastructure is precisely that: to support, enable, and foster research for which discovery of information is critical. In particular, we have hopes that rare materials will be findable and that a series of small collections may form a critical mass of information that may be highly relevant to various small science fields, such as ethnography and cultural linguistics, in which the projects have traditionally been carried out by individual investigators, and the research collections frequently end up in archives, where they may be perceived more in terms of their biographical value than in terms of current science. In this sense, the hidden collections effort is similar to the institutional repository movement, in which, again, research collections of students and faculty are collected and preserved at the local level but can be found, reused, and repurposed in future investigations that draw on multiple collections.

I recognize that discovering and repurposing small collections that are widely distributed over many institutions is more a dream than a reality, and much needs to change before that vision becomes commonplace: We will need agreed-upon and interoperable metadata, distributed search engines, tools and policies to support depositing so that archiving truly does begin at creation, plus a mind set among researchers that appreciates the value of preserved information for current research, and for research designs that rely on access to such information rather than on newly collected data. Our vision requires a cultural change in the way that much science is done. But change in the conduct of research is afoot, and attaining the vision speaks to CLIR's purpose: to clarify the issues, ask hard questions, convene the right people in the right room at the right time to articulate and pursue common causes, and in the end to do our part in the long transformation of higher education and advanced research in which we find ourselves. At CLIR, we work with a very broad range of people, from library directors and chief information officers at small liberal arts colleges, who balance the costs of a new roof for the gymnasium against investments in the IT infrastructure, to senior researchers at the basic science research agencies, who envisage possibilities 30 years from today. Although my head may be in the clouds and my heart in research, my boots, like CLIR's, are always on the ground.

Notes

NB: Internet addresses in the following notes and references were accurate as of December 2008 unless otherwise indicated.

1. Pew Internet and American Life Project, "April 8–May 11, 2008 Tracking Survey. N=2,251 Adults, 18 and Older. Margin of Error Is 2% for Results Based on the Full Sample and 3% for Results Based on Internet Users," October 19, 2008, http://www.pewinternet .org/Reports/2008/Use-of-Cloud-Computing-Applications-and-Services/Questions-and-Data. aspx?r=1. As of mid-August 2008, 21.9 percent of the world's population had some form of Internet access, a three-fold increase since 2000. Internet penetration, an unlovely term that measures the proportion of a population with access to the net, was highest in North America (73.6 percent), followed by Oceania/Australia (59.5 percent), and Europe (48.1 percent). But growth in the same eight-year period was fastest in the Middle East (1,176.8 percent), Africa (1,031.2 percent), and Latin America/Caribbean (669.3 percent); see "World Internet Usage Statistics News and World Population Stats," August 8, 2008, http://www.internetworldstats.com/stats.htm (accessed August 2008). Note that the top three languages in use on the Web are English, Chinese, and Spanish; see "Top Ten Internet Languages—World Internet Statistics," 1st quarter 2008, http://www.internetworldstats.com/stats7.htm. All Internet addresses above were accurate as of February 20, 2009.

2. U.S. National Science Foundation, Cyberinfrastructure Council, *Cyberinfrastructure Vision for 21st Century Discovery*, March 2007, 6, http://www.nsf.gov/pubs/2007/nsf0728/ index.jsp (accessed February 20, 2009).

3. American Council of Learned Societies, Commission on Cyberinfrastructure for the Humanities and Social Sciences, *Our Cultural Commonwealth*, 2007, http://www.acls.org/ cyberinfrastructure/OurCulturalCommonwealth.pdf (accessed February 20, 2009).

4. Research Council, UK, "E-Science: About the U.K. e-Science Programme," October 19, 2008, http://www.rcuk.ac.uk/escience/default.htm.

5. Association of Research Libraries, *Agenda for Developing E-Science in Research Libraries; ARL Joint Task Force on Library Support for E-Science Final Report & Recommendations*, November 2007, 6, http://www.arl.org/bm~doc/ARL_EScience_final.pdf. Also see Wikipedia, The Free Encyclopedia, "E-Science," ID: 242158553 1 October 2008 03:42 UTC, http://en.wikipedia .org/wiki/E-Science.

6. Christopher Greer, "E-Science: Trends, Transformations & Responses," ARL & CNI Forum on Reinventing Science Librarianship: Models for the Future, October 15, 2008, slide 5, document provided to author by Dr. Greer and used with his permission.

7. The State of São Paulo Research Foundation, "Four Decades of Research," http://www .fapesp.br/english/materia/35/background/four-decades-of-research.htm.

8. Human Resources Department, European Organization for Nuclear Research, "CERN Personnel Statistics 2006," March 2007, https://hr-info.web.cern.ch/hr-info/stats/persstats/ CERNPersonnelStatistics2006.pdf (accessed February 20, 2009).

9. European Organization for Nuclear Research, "CERN—the LHC Experiments," 2008. Available at: http://public.web.cern.ch/Public/en/LHC/LHCExperiments-en.html. European Organization for Nuclear Research, "Atlas: A Toroidal LHC ApparatuS," 2008, http://public.web.cern.ch/Public/en/LHC/ATLAS-en.html. European Organization for Nuclear Research, "LHCf: Large Hadron Collider forward," 2008, http://public.web.cern.ch/Public/en/LHC/LHCf-en.html.

10. Note that this single set of databases is unitary from the perspective of content; the databases themselves may be replicated and mirrored in several locations to afford access and to enhance security of the content.

11. U.S. National Science Foundation, *Cyberinfrastructure Vision for 21st Century Discovery*, chap. 3: "Data, Data Analysis, and Visualization (2006–2010)," http://nsf.gov/pubs/2007/nsf0728/index.jsp. Christine Borgman elaborates on this point in her recent monograph: *Scholarship in the Digital Age* (Cambridge, MA: MIT Press, 2007), especially chap. 6, "Data: Input and Output of Scholarship."

12. Joel M. Smith and Jared L. Cohon, "Managing the Digital Ecosystem, Information Technology and the Research University," *Issues in Science and Technology* (Fall 2005), http://www.issues.org/22.1/smith.html.

13. Roger Schonfeld and Kevin M. Guthrie, "The Changing Information Services Needs of Faculty," *Educause Review* 42, no. 4 (July/August 2007): 8–9, http://connect.educause.edu/library/EDUCAUSE+Review/TheChangingInformationSer/44598.

14. *No Brief Candle: Reconceiving Research Libraries for the 21st Century* (Washington, D.C.: Council on Library and Information Resources, August 2008).

15. Office of Cyberinfrastructure, U.S. National Science Foundation, "Sustainable Digital Data Preservation and Access Network Partners (DataNet)," http://www.nsf.gov/funding/pgm_summ.jsp?pims_id=503141.

16. John F. Gantz, Chrisopher Chute, Alex Manfrediz, Stephen Minton et al., *The Diverse and Exploding Digital Universe; an Updated Forecast of Worldwide Information Growth through 2011* (Framington, MA: IDC, 2008), 2–4.

17. Kenneth Flamm, Amy Friedlander, John Horrigan et al., *Measuring Broadband: Improving Communications Policymaking through Better Data Collection* (Washington, D.C.: Pew Internet and American Life Project, 2007), 19, 22, http://www.pewinternet.org/Reports/2007/Measuring-Broadband.aspx?r=1.

18. Gregory Crane and Amy Friedlander, *Many More than a Million: Building the Digital Environment for the Age of Abundance* (Washington, D.C.: CLIR, 2008), http://www.clir.org/activities/digitalscholar/Nov28final.pdf.

19. Winston Tabb, "'Wherefore Are These Things Hid?' A Report of a Survey Undertaken by the ARL Special Collections Task Force," *RBM* (Fall 2004) 5, no. 2:123–26, http://www.ala.org/ala/mgrps/divs/acrl/publications/rbm/5-2/tabb.pdf

PART III

PERSPECTIVES FROM INDIVIDUAL RESEARCH LIBRARIES

CHAPTER 7

E-SCIENCE AT JOHNS HOPKINS UNIVERSITY

G. Sayeed Choudhury

This chapter describes prominent E-science initiatives at Johns Hopkins University (JHU), which has established a leadership position in E-science through several projects and initiatives, many of which have benefited from the Sloan Digital Sky Survey (SDSS). While digital astronomy represents a forefront discipline, the E-science initiatives at JHU have expanded into several other disciplines including environmental science, turbulence research, medical sciences, and library and information sciences. The E-science initiatives at JHU have been organized into the Institute for Data Intensive Engineering and Science (IDIES). As the IDIES charter document indicates:

> A unique opportunity exists to coalesce data-intensive science efforts at Johns Hopkins into a well-focused center of activity, which would then propel various fields towards new discoveries and breakthroughs.[1]

IDIES brings together the academic divisions and libraries at JHU into a cohesive partnership, reflecting the need for a comprehensive vision and strategy across the university. In addition to research activities, a core component of IDIES relates to the integration of E-science into the educational and curriculum development at JHU. Each academic division and the libraries will provide shared financial support,

The work described in this article is supported through an Institute of Museum and Library Services National Leadership Grant (LG0606018206) and a grant from Microsoft Corporation. In addition, the NVO and Teragrid have committed funding to this work. While several individuals have participated in this work, I am especially indebted to Alex Szalay, Bob Hanisch, and Tim DiLauro for the specific ideas noted in this article.

staff, and equipment resources. In addition, IDIES has planned to convene a series of meetings to highlight JHU E-science and to engage the broader community.

The first section of this chapter describes the SDSS and the National Virtual Observatory (NVO), two digital astronomy projects that have influenced E-science at JHU and beyond. The second section describes the application of the SDSS tools into other scientific domains, a development that is indicative of early stages of broader infrastructure development. The third section describes the central and expanding role of the JHU library in the E-science landscape at JHU. The final section contains observations and conclusions.

Sloan Digital Sky Survey and National Virtual Observatory

The SDSS[2] is one of the most well-known and cited E-science projects. It began in 1992 and acquired its final data in May 2008. While SDSS involved several institutions and individuals, Professor Alexander Szalay from the Department of Physics and Astronomy at JHU has played a leadership role. SDSS transformed astronomy research and generated new outreach and educational opportunities, including opportunities for amateur or "citizen scientists." Sometimes referred to as the "Cosmic Genome Project," SDSS resulted in 40 terabytes of publicly available data, 5 terabytes of processed catalogs, and 2.5 terapixels of images. There are 1,600 peer-reviewed publications that cite SDSS data. SDSS had the world's most utilized astronomy facility in 2006 and 2007 (Szalay 2008, personal communication). In addition, there have been over 425 million hits in six years to the SkyServer[3] Web site that provides access to the SDSS data. There are about 930,000 distinct users even though there are only about 10,000 professional astronomers in the world. SDSS has delivered over 50,000 hours of lecture materials for high schools. Recently, the SDSS team launched Galaxy Zoo,[4] an online resource that allows anyone to participate in the classification of galaxies within images. Galaxy Zoo has attracted a broad community of about 100,000 people who also produce blogs and even poems about astronomy! Through Galaxy Zoo, a schoolteacher in the Netherlands recently made a discovery about a previously undocumented astronomical object.

The NVO[5] is a community-wide effort "to enable new science by greatly enhancing access to data and computing resources. NVO makes it easy to locate, retrieve, and analyze data from archives and catalogs worldwide." NVO has developed a set of standards, based on the Flexible Image Transport System[6] format, that support interoperability or data access between different digital astronomy projects (Hanisch 2007). Astronomers can now access and analyze data sets from a diverse array of resources through common interfaces and tools. Similar to SDSS, the NVO also features an extensive set of resources for outreach and education, such as the NVO Summer School. The NVO has inspired 15 other NVO efforts that are coordinated by the International Virtual Observatory Alliance.[7]

Arguably, there are certain characteristics of digital astronomy that support the development of such community-wide resources and services. For example, astronomy data do not have privacy concerns, commercial value, or legal restrictions in ways that other disciplinary data may have. Additionally, astronomy projects typically acquire data through a small number of instruments (e.g., one telescope) such that it is easier to introduce systematic data practices or procedures. Nonetheless, SDSS and NVO have not only revolutionized astronomy research and education; they have provided "blueprints" for other E-science projects and communities.

Technology Transfer

Through collaborative efforts based at JHU, the underlying technology and the framework of the SkyServer have been applied to new projects such as the Life Under Your Feet soil-ecology resource,[8] the JHU Turbulence Database Cluster,[9] and the OncoSpace Project. The application of database technology and Web services has proven particularly useful. These "technology transfer" activities demonstrate that despite differences in disciplines (i.e., astronomy, environmental sciences, turbulence research, radiation oncology) and in data acquisition modes, data types, and data management practices, there is common technology that may be applied across them. These applications of technology result in unforeseen similarities in research practices or approaches. The latest example relates to astronomy and radiation oncology through the OncoSpace project at JHU. OncoSpace aims to aggregate the entire medical history of patients and their treatments with time series information using the SkyServer framework. Astronomers and radiation oncologists believe there are similarities to the NVO in the sense that each patient is like a "galaxy" observed by many different instruments, at different wavelengths, with data stored at different locations.

These developments are consistent with historical trends of infrastructure development. A report from a workshop sponsored in part by the U.S. National Science Foundation states that infrastructure eventually becomes "ubiquitous, accessible, reliable, and transparent" as it matures (Edwards et al. 2007). At earlier stages, however, the pattern is different:

> The initial stage in infrastructure formation is system-building, characterized by the deliberate and successful design of technology-based services. Next, technology transfer across domains and locations results in variations on the original design, as well as the emergence of competing systems. Infrastructures typically form only when these various systems merge, in a process of consolidation characterized by gateways that allow dissimilar systems to be linked into networks.

It is reasonable to assert that SkyServer represents a system that was developed to meet a specific disciplinary need, and the application to projects in other disciplines represents an example of this type of technology transfer. As JHU's E-science systems migrate into infrastructure, there is an increasing emphasis on persistent, cross-disciplinary access to data. Given libraries' historical expertise with long-term archiving, and the specific skills of the Digital Research and Curation Center (DRCC), the Sheridan Libraries at JHU have become an important partner in E-science initiatives.

Data Curation

As the SDSS and NVO projects acquired data and moved toward the end of their first phases, the project leaders realized that they needed a plan and infrastructure for long-term data curation. The DRCC[10] defines curation as "maintaining and adding value to a trusted body of digital information for current and future use; specifically, we mean the active management and appraisal of data over the life-cycle of scholarly and scientific materials."

The DRCC is a research and development facility within the Sheridan Libraries at JHU. The DRCC, previously known as the Digital Knowledge Center, has secured grants through the National Science Foundation, Institute of Museum and Library Services, the Library of Congress, the Andrew W. Mellon Foundation, and private sector sources such as Microsoft. The DRCC includes individuals with backgrounds in computer science, engineering, cognitive science, mathematics, and geology. Through these grants and its diverse staff, the DRCC developed expertise and knowledge of data curation that proved useful for the SDSS and NVO. The combination of a research-and-development facility within the stable, persistent organizational framework of a library provides an important, and perhaps unique, organizational dimension that is noteworthy in the context of data curation.

JHU's initial data-curation initiative focused on the NVO for a few reasons. While the NVO fostered greater interoperability and use of data from various sources, it did not explicitly consider the long-term curation of data. The NVO typically deals with the smaller-sized, high-level, or refined data sets such as the ones that are typically cited within publications. These data are more readily managed than the larger, "raw," less refined data (e.g., data directly generated from telescopes). Additionally, there are existing mechanisms for at least storing and backing up the raw data through centralized astronomy facilities, but the refined data are not being captured systematically. The DRCC's previous research has focused on ingest or "import" of large (at least by library standards) data sets into repositories and integration of these repositories with applications such as electronic publishing systems. All of these elements led to a project to develop an end-to-end prototype system that will capture high-level digital data as part of the publication process and establish a distributed network of curated, permanent data repositories (Choudhury et al. 2007). The data in this network will be accessible through the research journals, astronomy data centers, and NVO data-discovery portals. The partners for this prototype development effort include the NVO, research libraries, the American Astronomical Society (AAS), and its publishing partner.

The high-level architecture for this prototype data-curation system involves a publication and editorial process that will include data capture, metadata tagging, and linking between digital data and journal articles using persistent identifiers. A data storage appliance based on the Fedora repository software will handle the data ingest or import. The Sheridan Libraries will develop these appliances and help install them at partner libraries at the University of Washington and the University of Edinburgh. Publishers, the AAS, or NVO sites could also host these data appliances.

The astronomy data will be replicated among these data appliances for redundancy, and the VOSpace environment for distributed storage will provide authentication and authorization services for data sets that may have restricted access. Data access will be provided from journal articles or through the NVO. Finally, research libraries and journal editorial staff will be involved with metadata curation through direct interaction with a metadata database.

Recently, the DRCC has developed a data model of a typical astronomy article using the Open Archives Initiative Object Reuse and Exchange specification.[11] ORE has been developed specifically to address compound digital objects that have constituent elements distributed across repositories. The astronomy data and articles will be described using aggregations and resource maps. The model provides citation links between articles, a connection between data and articles, and a provenance chain through which one can trace the origin of data from varying levels of processing or refinement at different stages of a project. The data model explicitly acknowledges the changing nature of scientific publications and of research that is increasingly data-intensive.

Conclusions

In the same way that the SkyServer framework and technology were transferred into other E-science projects, the data curation work with the NVO is being considered by other disciplines. The Optical Society of America, which deals with brain science data and articles, has expressed an interest in adopting the framework of the NVO data-curation prototype system. Additionally, as the SDSS project reaches the conclusion of its first phase, the project leadership has started a dialogue with the libraries at JHU and the University of Chicago about curating the entire SDSS data, which include nearly 100 terabytes of diverse content. Fundamentally, as libraries develop greater expertise with data curation, it is reasonable to assume that an increasing number of E-science projects will request support from them for long-term preservation and access to data. Choudhury (2008) outlines the important lessons that have been gained through the interaction of the NVO and Sheridan Libraries at JHU. These important lessons relate to the changing nature of research, publications, and new roles for libraries. However, the most important lesson relates to the human dimensions of E-science. Collaboration is built on trust that takes time to develop—and technology does not create trust. Successful E-science infrastructure will require both technology and human components that work together.

Notes

NB: Internet addresses in the notes and references below were accurate as of January 11, 2008.

1. http://idies.jhu.edu.
2. http://www.sdss.org/.

3. http://cas.sdss.org/dr6/en/.
4. http://galaxyzoo.org/.
5. http://www.us-vo.org.
6. http://heasarc.nasa.gov/docs/heasarc/fits.html.
7. http://www.ivoa.net/.
8. http://lifeunderyourfeet.org/en/default.asp. Also see Szlavecz et al. 2006 in references below.
9. http://turbulence.pha.jhu.edu/. Also see Li et al. 2008 in references below.
10. http://www.dcc.ac.uk/.
11. http://www.openarchives.org/ore/. Also see Van de Sompel et al. 2006 in references below.

References

Choudhury, G. S. 2008. "The Virtual Observatory Meets the Library." *Journal of Electronic Publishing* 11, no. 1. http://quod.lib.umich.edu/cgi/t/text/text-idx?c=jep;cc=jep;rgn=main;view=text;idno=3336451.0011.111.

Choudhury, G. S., T. DiLauro, A. Szalay, E. Vishniac, R. J. Hanisch, and J. Steffen. 2007. "Digital Data Preservation for Scholarly Publications in Astronomy." *International Journal of Digital Curation* 2, no. 2. http://www.ijdc.net/index.php/ijdc/article/view/41.

Edwards, P. N., S. J. Jackson, G. C. Bowker, and C. P. Knobel, eds. 2007. "Understanding Infrastructure: Dynamics, Tension, and Design." Report of a Workshop on History and Lessons for New Scientific Cyberinfrastructures. http://hdl.handle.net/2027.42/49353.

Hanisch, R. J. 2007. "The Virtual Observatory: Core Capabilities and Support for Statistical Analyses in Astronomy." In *Statistical Challenges in Modern Astronomy IV*, ed. G. J. Babu and E. D. Feigelson, 177. San Francisco, CA: Astronomical Society of the Pacific, ASP Conf. Ser., 371.

Li, Y., E. Perlman, M. Yan, Y. Yang, R. Burns, C. Meneveau, S. Chen, A. Szalay, and G. Eyink. 2008. "A Public Turbulence Database Cluster and Applications to Study Lagrangian Evolution of Velocity Increments in Turbulence." *Journal of Turbulence* 9, no. 31:1–29, http://www.yikes.com/~eric/papers/Lietal08.pdf.

Szlavecz, K. A., A. Terzis, S. Ozer, R. Muscăloiu-E, J. Cogan, S. Small, R. Burns, J. Gray, and A. Szalay. 2006. Life under Your Feet: An End-to-End Soil Ecology Sensor Network, Database, Web Server, and Analysis Service. Microsoft Research. http://research.microsoft.com/research/pubs/view.aspx?msr_tr_id=MSR-TR-2006-90.

Van de Sompel, H., C. Lagoze, J. Bekaert, X. Liu, S. Payette, and S. Warner. 2006. "An Interoperable Fabric for Scholarly Value Chains." *D-Lib Magazine* 12, no. 10. http://www.dlib.org/dlib/october06/vandesompel/10vandesompel.html.

CHAPTER 8

An Idiosyncratic Perspective on the History and Development at University California, San Diego, of Support for Cyberinfrastructure-Enabled E-Science

Brian E. C. Schottlaender

On Terminology

I have heard it said that E-science and cyberinfrastructure are, or can be, used interchangeably. I have likewise heard it said that E-science is used in Europe, whereas cyberinfrastructure is used in the United States; and, again, they are used to mean the same thing. In this chapter, they will not be used interchangeably or to mean the same thing.

In Wikipedia Cyberinfrastructure is described as being:

> The new research environments that support advanced data acquisition, data storage, data management, data integration, data mining, data visualization and other computing and information processing services over the Internet. In scientific usage, cyberinfrastructure is a technological solution to the problem of efficiently connecting data, computers, and people with the goal of enabling derivation of novel scientific theories and knowledge.[1]

Wikipedia also quotes Dr. Francine Berman, director of the San Diego Supercomputer Center (SDSC), as describing Cyberinfrastructure to be

The author is grateful to his UCSD colleagues Francine Berman, Luc Declerck, and Mike Norman for their contributions to this paper.

the coordinated aggregate of software, hardware and other technologies, as well as human expertise, required to support current and future discoveries in science and engineering. The challenge of Cyberinfrastructure is to integrate relevant and often disparate resources to provide a useful, usable, and enabling framework for research and discovery characterized by broad access and "end-to-end" coordination.[2]

Ironically, Wikipedia also observes that "Cyberinfrastructure is also called e-Science."[3]

E-science, on the other hand, is described in Wikipedia as being

computationally intensive science that is carried out in highly distributed network environments, or science that uses immense data sets that require grid computing; the term sometimes includes technologies that enable distributed collaboration.[4]

Here too, Wikipedia notes that, in the United States, "the term cyberinfrastructure is typically used to define e-Science projects."[5]

It is easy enough to understand—what with embedded phrases like "distributed network environments," "grid computing," and "technologies that enable distributed collaboration"—why E-science and cyberinfrastructure are used interchangeably, if not confused. To do so, however, ignores the critical enabling relationship between the two concepts: that is, cyberinfrastructure is the means to the end that is E-science. The latter cannot, quite literally, be carried out without the former; and without the latter, the former is little more than a solution in search of a problem. Thus, in this chapter, when I am speaking of the means, I'll use cyberinfrastructure; when of the end, E-science.

Early History: SDSC, 1985–2004

Until recently, the primary manifestation of cyberinfrastructure support for E-science at the University of California, San Diego (UCSD), was the SDSC, which was created jointly in 1985 by UCSD and General Atomics, with primary funding from the U.S. National Science Foundation (NSF). Located on the UCSD campus, SDSC operated as a division of General Atomics until 1997, with a research focus on earthquakes, global climate, and other scientific subjects requiring massive "compute" power. When NSF's Supercomputer Center Program came to an end in 1997, SDSC—whose computers had an aggregate capacity of 270 gigaflops, as compared with the 25–30 gigaflop capacity of other computing clusters on the UCSD campus[6]—became an Organized Research Unit (ORU) of UCSD.

In 1996 NSF launched the PACI Program (Partnerships for Advanced Computational Infrastructure) and in 1997 SDSC was named by NSF one of two national leading-edge sites (the other was NCSA, the National Center for Supercomputing Applications, led at the time by Dr. Larry Smarr, at the University of Illinois). In addition to compute-intensive hardware, the focus of the PACI program was on partnership, community building, and integrative software.[7]

The cyberinfrastructure assembled at SDSC over the course of this virtually unprecedented 20 years of growth included as of 2005

- 400 professionals with expertise across multiple scientific domains and computing technologies;
- DataStar, initially a 10.4-teraflops supercomputer ranked among the 25 top supercomputers in the world;
- an IBM Blue Gene eServer architecture that combines high processor performance with low power consumption;
- six petabytes of archival tape storage and 500 terabytes of online disk storage; and
- locally developed data management software, including the Storage Resource Broker (SRB).[8]

The E-science supported by this constellation of resources includes

- Alliance for Cell Signaling (AFCS);[9]
- Biomedical Informatics Research Network (BIRN);[10]
- Cooperative Association for Internet Data Analysis (CAIDA);[11]
- Cyberinfrastructure for Phylogenetic Research (CiPRES);[12]
- Geosciences Network (GEON);[13]
- High Performance Wireless Research and Education Network (HPWREN);[14]
- Network for Earthquake Engineering Simulation (NEES);[15]
- National Ecological Observatory Network (NEON);[16]
- National Laboratory for Applied Network Research (NLANR);[17]
- Ocean Research Interactive Observatory Networks (ORION), now Ocean Observatories Initiative (OOI);[18]
- Protein Data Bank (PDB);[19]
- Plant Genome Research Program (PLANTS);[20]
- Real-time Observatories, Applications, and Data Management Network (ROADNet); and[21]
- Science Environment for Ecological Knowledge (SEEK).[22]

Modern History (Part I): SDSC, 2005–Present

In 2004 the PACI program was terminated and NSF, instead, provided SDSC and NCSA sufficient "core funding" to continue them as Cyberinfrastructure Centers through 2007, the intended conclusion date for PACI. Among the differences between the formal (in NSF terms) "Cyberinfrastructure Era" that is now upon us and the data science ecosystem that preceded it is this: in the new era, "enabling technologies must be coordinated, integrated, usable, and interoperable"[23] in order to meet the varying needs of multiple domains and user communities. Also the present ecosystem includes players in addition to the supercomputer centers, the private investigators, and the federal funding agencies that had previously populated it, along with libraries and university academic and administrative computing centers. Moreover, the

present environment is suffused with far greater anxiety about, and consequent attention to, data access issues, both in the public policy arena and in the preservation and
archiving arena. Finally, there are far fewer financial resources available at present, or at
least far greater competition for those resources. All of these factors have had, and will
have, implications for SDSC, the shape that cyberinfrastructure support at UCSD is
taking, the ends to which that infrastructure will be put, and the financial and organizational models likely needed to achieve those ends.

Between the succession of Francine Berman to the SDSC directorship in 2001 and
the demise of the PACI Program in 2004, SDSC focused increasingly on establishing
collaborative relationships on the UCSD campus, including partnerships with the
UCSD Libraries (UCSDL) and the California Institute of Information Technology
and Telecommunications (Calit2), directed by Dr. Larry Smarr, formerly of NCSA.
Both the UCSDL and Calit2 are in the information business, if not the knowledge
business, and SDSC's partnership overtures make clear its realization that it is no longer just in the computing business, but is in the same information business as well.

What, in fact, the three campus agencies have in common is data. In 2005, SDSC was
reviewed by UCSD (as are all of UCSD's ORUs, periodically). In that review, Berman
noted that during the period 2006–2010 the center would provide "professional-level
data services, software, and curation beyond what is feasible in university/campus/
research lab facilities, and not available in the private sector," adding that "this focus is
also helping us diversify SDSC's funding portfolio, adding data-oriented projects and
funding from NIH, the Library of Congress, the National Archives, the museum and
library communities, and others, in addition to our traditional support from NSF."[24]

Campus and System Context

In the last several years, a variety of conversations on- and off-campus have helped
shape UC San Diego's commitment to supporting E-science. In 2002, then-UCSD
Chancellor Robert Dynes constituted and charged a campus-wide Technology
Directions Committee, chaired by Dr. Sid Karin, former (and founding) director
of the SDSC. During its three years of existence, the committee explored a variety
of technology-related themes.

I chaired the subcommittee that led the group's deliberations in regard to content.
The following questions informed our thinking:

- What intellectual assets do we have?
- How do/could they add value to what we do/want to do?
- What facilitates/would facilitate their adding that value?[25]

In colloquial terms, the third question was answered as follows:

- place(s) to put them
- tools for getting them there
- standards for encoding/describing them

- tools for discovering them
- tools for manipulating them
- tools for sharing them
- tools for protecting them[26]

The group concluded that the infrastructure necessary to satisfy the "requirements" in bullets above would need to include the following:

- institutional repository(ies)
- preservation repository(ies)
- metadata registry(ies)
- discovery interfaces
- security/use protocol
- migration/preservation strategies[27]

All of these cyberinfrastructure components are now either developed or in development.

When current UCSD Chancellor Marye Anne Fox arrived in 2005, she instituted an annual series of senior management retreats intended to foster discussion of the most pressing issues facing the campus, data stewardship among them. In this context, the use not of the word *management*—"the conducting or supervising of something (as a business)"[28]—but rather of the word *stewardship*—"the careful and responsible management of something entrusted to one's care"[29]—is significant for two reasons. First, rhetorically, *stewardship* suggests greater attention or even empathy than does *management*. *Stewardship* is careful, responsible, entrusted. Second, and less obviously, *stewardship* signifies the campus's growing recognition that there is more to data curation than simple "bit" management—that, indeed, data curation is rather more in the nature of a custodial suite of services and policies than of a managerial one.

At the UC San Diego Chancellor's Retreat of 2006, Berman and I were asked to articulate the needs of the campus with regard to data stewardship. We noted that these assets were increasingly at risk, whether as a consequence of resource scarcity, technology evolution (including evolution of storage and delivery systems, access mechanisms, and encoding formats), calamity, or inaction. We went on to describe a then-unique partnership (now, less rare) between the SDSC and the UCSDL—a partnership planned and poised to mitigate the risks described above. More on that partnership shortly.

In parallel with these campus-level discussions, in 2006 University of California Provost Wyatt R. (Rory) Hume charged a system-wide Information Technology Guidance Committee (ITGC) "to engage in a consultative, 18-month systemwide planning process to

- identify strategic directions for IT investments that enable campuses to meet their distinctive needs more effectively while supporting the university's broader mission, academic programs and strategic goals;

- promote the deployment of information technology services to support innovation and the enhancement of academic quality and institutional competitiveness;
- leverage IT investment and expertise to fully exploit collective and campus-specific IT capabilities."[30]

The ITGC had the following six focus areas, each with an expert working group:

- advanced networking services
- common IT architecture
- high performance research computing
- instructional technology
- IT in student experience
- stewardship of digital assets (The working group on this I chaired.)

Tellingly, the final report of the ITGC, submitted in December 2007, is titled "Creating a UC Cyberinfrastructure." The report states unequivocally that "Development of a University of California[-wide] cyberinfrastructure is critical to our success."[31] The report contains only nine recommendations, a seemingly modest number:

1. Establish the IT Leadership Council as the UC-wide IT governing body "in close collaboration with academic and administrative leaders at both the campus and systemwide levels."
2. Fund IT as critical infrastructure; "change current funding models to provide sustainable, renewable funding."
3. Apply proven collaboration models; "collaboration is the way forward."
4. Invest in network connectivity "by continually expanding network bandwidth and computing capabilities."
5. Plan for the next-generation UC data center infrastructure; "develop a new blueprint for providing scalable data center services to the UC community."
6. Develop IT infrastructure, tools, and services to support collaboration within the UC community.
7. Develop UC Grid research cyberinfrastructure services; "deliver reliable, robust high-performance computing services and tools to research faculty who do not need (or cannot afford) to manage their own."
8. Create the capacity to manage our digital assets "by adopting strategies to ensure that the information produced in the course of research and instruction is effectively secured, managed, preserved, and made available for appropriate use."
9. Cultivate organizational leadership for instructional technology and IT in the student experience, "providing learners with enhanced and new IT-enabled educational opportunities."[32]

Even a cursory reading, however, reveals these recommendations to be a much taller order than their relatively sparse number might suggest.

Modern History (Part II): SDSC and UCSDL

The mission of SDSC is to "innovate, develop, and use technology to advance science,"[33] while that of the UCSDL is to "be leaders in providing and promoting information resources and services to the UCSD community when, where, and how users want them."[34] What is it that these two missions have in common? Each implies the need for substantial curation and preservation infrastructure. As the information environment in which each organization operates has become increasingly data-rich, the institutions involved have become increasingly aware that leveraging investments made by each will redound not only to the benefit of both but to that of the larger organization within which they both operate, namely UCSD.

SDSC and UCSDL began partnering on data-intensive projects in 2001 when, joined by the Scripps Institution of Oceanography, they successfully competed for one of the NSDL I grants (National Science Digital Library, Round I). They repeated that success in 2003 when, again with Scripps, they won an NSDL II grant (National Science Digital Library, Round II). Both of those initiatives called for the development of tools and services that facilitate the ingesting and management of data and publications arising from, or incorporating, those data. Both initiatives also involved the build-out of the SRB, which is SDSC-developed middleware that "supports shared collections that can be distributed across multiple organizations and heterogeneous storage systems."[35] SRB has several distinguishing features including: (1) it is agnostic as to content type and format, and (2) it "containerizes" data. This latter feature is a particularly compelling one because it allows various curatorial activities (e.g., ingestion, organization, discovery, access control) to be carried out at the container level, reducing in the process the various overheads associated with having to carry out these activities more atomically.

Since entering into those initiatives, SDSC has collaborated ever more closely and deliberately not only with the UCSDL but with other libraries as well at the regional and national levels. At the local level, the UCSDL have used an SRB instance as the basis for developing our own Digital Asset Management System (DAMS). Once an object collection is identified, the Metadata Analysis and Specification Unit of the UCSDL creates an assembly plan, maps data to MODS, PREMIS, MIX, or various local schemas as necessary, and ingests the collection into the SRB. Original digital objects, their technical metadata, and their descriptive metadata are all stored in the SRB. The UCSDL DAMS currently has six terabytes of content under active management, including texts, images (still and moving), and sound files. The libraries have begun discussions with campus academic colleagues about bringing data archives under curatorial management as well.

At the UC system-wide level, SDSC and the California Digital Library (CDL) are partnering to manage the CDL's Digital Preservation Repository (DPR). In addition to providing back-end storage for the DPR, SDSC is collaborating with CDL on the so-called Mass Transit project, an initiative to "better understand issues in large-scale transfer and replication of data in the context of digital preservation ... [whose]

primary deliverables will include extensive data-transfer tests and a publicly available, jointly authored CDL/SDSC document on best practices and situation-based recommendations for institutions embarking on large data-transfer in the context of preservation."[36] The DPR is currently scaled to accommodate forty terabytes of content under active management.

This latter project is but one example of UCSD's growing leadership in the arena of long-term digital data preservation. Chronopolis—a collaborative project between SDSC, the UCSDL, the U.S. National Center for Atmospheric Research (NCAR), and the University of Maryland—is another.

The Preservation Imperative

A report on long-lived digital data collections, published by the U.S. National Science Board in 2005, stated that "long-lived digital data collections are powerful catalysts for progress and for democratization of science and education."[37] It defined data as

> any information that can be stored in digital form, including text, numbers, images, video or movies, audio, software, algorithms, equations, animations, models, simulations, etc. Such data may be generated by various means including observation, computation, or experiment.[38]

The publication went on to describe "long-lived" as extending for a period of time "long enough for there to be concern about the impacts of changing technology."[39] Finally, while the concluding exhortation in the report is directed specifically to the NSF, it represents a call to action for us all:

> Given the proliferation of resource and reference collections and the costs associated with creating and maintaining them, it is imperative that the Foundation develop a comprehensive strategy—incorporating and integrating technical and financial considerations—for long-lived data collections and determine the steps necessary to anticipate future needs.[40]

UC San Diego has not only heeded that call; we—and our partners—may well have had a hand in prompting it.

In 2004, SDSC, UCSDL, NCAR, and the University of Maryland did something highly unusual: we submitted an unsolicited proposal to the NSF titled "Chronopolis: Federated Digital Preservation Across Time and Space." The proposal's project summary read as follows:

> There is a critical need to organize, preserve, and make accessible the increasing number of digital holdings that represent intellectual capital. This intellectual capital contains scientific records that are the basis for current research, future scientific advances, and education source materials for use by the public, educators, scientists and engineers

now and for the foreseeable future. We propose a national center for the management, long-term preservation, and promulgation of national digital assets, Chronopolis.

Chronopolis will provide a model facility that enables long-term support of irreplaceable and important national data collections, ensuring that: (1) Standard reference datasets remain available to provide critical science reference material; (2) Collections can expand and evolve over time, as well as weather evolution in the underlying technologies; and (3) Preservation "of last resort" is available for critical disciplinary and interdisciplinary digital resources at risk of being lost.

Chronopolis will provide tools, software, and services needed to manage data, information, and knowledge at the scales required for national digital holdings. It will function as a distributed national "data backbone," federating data and information (preservation over "space"), and will provide operational data services for maintaining key digital collections for the long term, ranging from scientific databases to library holdings (preservation over "time"). Chronopolis will integrate a production system with a research and development laboratory, and an administration and policy team to provide a scalable model for Cyberinfrastructure data management evolution and long-term preservation.[41]

While the foundation did not fund the proposal, it clearly got foundation officials, or their governing board, thinking.

Undeterred, SDSC and UCSDL submitted to NSF and the Library of Congress in 2005 a DigArch (Digital Archiving) proposal calling for:

demonstration of a software technology that will comprise . . . a preservation environment for a film/video collection that includes other related multi-media content such as audio, transcripts, annotations, related and introductory Web pages, and descriptive, technical, and rights metadata currently being captured in a FileMakerPro[TM] database . . . [an environment that would allow one to] take an existing video production workflow . . . being used for producing and Web-casting video content in a small-scale studio setting, and to integrate it with a digital preservation life-cycle management process that will enable the digital content to be archived for long-term preservation.[42]

The funded project allowed the partners to develop a long-term preservation system that could be inserted into an enterprise-grade television production cycle without disrupting that cycle. As a consequence, in two year's time, 300 hours of digital video were archived along with unedited footage, accompanying audio, transcripts, annotations, related Web pages, and production information.

In 2006, SDSC, UCSDL, and their partners at NCAR and the University of Maryland submitted a retooled version of the Chronopolis proposal to the National Digital Information Infrastructure and Preservation Program (NDIIPP) at the Library of Congress. Although specifically focused on NDIIPP data collections, this version of Chronopolis was very similar in its vision to that version proposed to NSF two years earlier: namely to provide "distributed storage, data replication, storage management, and core ingestion, curation, and preservation tools and services"[43] in support of digital data collections, stewarded under the aegis of NDIIPP. Data copies are reposited in three geographically-dispersed physical locations, linked by grid-enabled cyberinfrastructure under varying degrees of access control: bright, dim, and dark.[44] Moreover, any of the three sites can be bright, dim, or dark for a particular data collection. The funded project has two large collections—the social sciences data collection at the Interuniversity Consortium for Social and Political Research (which has 10 terabytes) and the CDL Web-At-Risk collection (25 terabytes)—under active management.

In 2007, the NSF issued its "DataNet" request for proposals (rfp), an ambitious rfp to create sustainable and extensible long-term preservation services needed to sustain the digital objects (broadly construed) that support science and engineering research and education. In addition, the rfp envisioned that this infrastructure would be managed and governed by "new types of organizations . . . [that] integrate library and archival sciences, cyberinfrastructure, computer and information sciences, and domain science expertise."[45] In a rushed and, I believe, ultimately divisive process, 27 preproposals were submitted, of which 17 were "qualified" for consideration, including a UCSD-led proposal titled "The Data Trust Alliance." Distressingly, UCSD's was not among the seven initiatives invited to submit full proposals. Only two of those initiatives will be funded in this round. Two or possibly three will be funded in a second round, although one will be required to start the process over from the beginning. UCSD has submitted a new, and decidedly different, proposal for consideration in this second round.

Looking Toward the Future

In 2007, UCSD—under the leadership of its Vice Chancellor for Research Art Ellis—assembled a campus working group to evaluate the future of, and possible future funding models for, SDSC in light of the fact that NSF core funding for the national supercomputing centers had come to an end. Represented on the group were Administrative Computing, Calit2, the UCSDL, SDSC, and various data-intensive academic domains (biology, engineering, medicine, oceanography, pharmacy). The working group's terms of reference included being charged to

- determine how the campus should envision the SDSC's role in the near future;
- develop a set of future scenarios and an evaluation of their strengths and weaknesses as potential blueprints for the future of SDSC; and
- be informed by SDSC's connections to other campus units, to the UC system, to the national laboratories, and to the broader national and international user community.[46]

Having observed that "success in the Information Age can be measured by the precision, power and breadth of available tools and the knowledge of the people who use them,"[47] the working group's report notes that SDSC provides the best of both. Of various future scenarios explored, the working group has come out in favor of "integration" at the programmatic level with various other campus agencies operating in the same space, noting that "if . . . carried out properly, UCSD is poised to become . . . [a]

national model for Research CI [cyberinfrastructure], given the collective partnering strengths of ACT, Calit2, SDSC, and the University Libraries."[48]

A separate CI Design Team (CIDT) has now been charged with imagining, assessing, and recommending the best technical architecture for effecting such an integration. The team comprises representatives from all major computing stakeholders on campus including SDSC, Academic Computing, Administrative Computing, Calit2, and the UCSDL. The CIDT began its work by surveying campus researchers in order to ascertain their unmet needs in the areas of computing, software, data management, networking, and cyberinfrastructure. A summary of the survey's most significant responses follows. Figures in parentheses show the percentage of researchers surveyed who expressed each need.

- Need for storage services
  - backup (88 percent)
  - capacity (70 percent)
- Interest in co-location (54 percent) and condo clusters (46 percent)
- Need for CI services
  - processing (70 percent)
  - system administration (48 percent)
  - cluster administration (38 percent)
- Need for CI expertise
  - database and data management (62 percent)
  - visualization (58 percent)
  - portals/user interfaces (55 percent)
- Need for software: Matlab, SPSS, iRODS, IDL, GIS (37 percent)[49]

In thinking about how to address these needs as effectively and efficiently as possible, the CIDT has been working on a technical architecture concept.[50]

In parallel with the work of the SDSC Working Group and the CIDT, Berman has been leading her management group through a strategic planning exercise, the intent of which is to imagine and articulate the shape of the "Next-Generation SDSC" (NGSDSC). NGSDSC is designed to accelerate cyberinfrastructure-enabled research and education efforts. Given a prevailing environment that features, on the one hand, "unlimited" data via the Internet, sensors, scientific instruments, and other tools, and, on the other hand, "unlimited" computation via university clusters, "compute clouds," terascale and petascale supercomputers, etc., SDSC is focusing on providing cyberinfrastructure services to empower researchers and educators to do something useful with these riches. Medium-term strategic directions of the center include the following:

- Cyberinfrastructure for emerging computational platforms
  - resources for large-scale data analysis
  - shared "condominium" clusters and power-efficient co-location facilities
  - support for the University of California Grid

- Comprehensive data cyberinfrastructure
  - data services
  - university-level archival repository and storage backbone
  - integrated data life-cycle management
- Innovation for next-generation cyberinfrastructure development and use
  - high performance computing on next-generation computing platforms
  - innovative environments for cloud platforms
  - green computing[51]

With the proper sorts of support, the three focused emphases above will combine to produce the "broad impact [and] deep-impact research CI"[52] needed to position SDSC, UCSD, and the University of California as continuing leaders in the development and management of cutting-edge technologies in service to the world's grandest scientific challenges.

"The proper sorts of support," in this context, are not simply financial. On the contrary, as noted by Dr. Berman at the outset of this chapter, cyberinfrastructure is a "coordinated aggregate." The "body of units . . . somewhat loosely associated with one another"[53] that constitute UCSD cyberinfrastructure organizationally— SDSC, Academic and Administrative Computing, Calit2, the Libraries—will need to work together like the components of a finely engineered timepiece if they are not only to succeed but to amount to more than the sum of their parts.

The next generation of cyberinfrastructure being planned and developed at SDSC and elsewhere is critical for addressing the next generation of E-science challenges. Reducing energy consumption, preventing infectious disease and managing pandemics, predicting earthquakes and tsunamis, mitigating threats to international security: all require the processing, management, and evaluation of massive amounts of data across vast distances and over very long periods of time. In short, all require cyberinfrastructure . . . and all are uppermost in the minds of today's researchers and universities.

Notes

NB: All Internet addresses below were accurate as of January 26, 2009.

1. http://en.wikipedia.org/wiki/Cyberinfrastructure.
2. Ibid.
3. Ibid.
4. http://en.wikipedia.org/wiki/EScience.
5. Ibid.
6. "San Diego Supercomputer Center ORU 5-Year Review," unpublished paper (2005), 3.
7. Ibid.
8. Ibid., 2.
9. http://www.afcs.org/.
10. http://www.nbirn.net/.

11. http://www.caida.org/home/.

12. http://www.phylo.org/.

13. http://www.geongrid.org/.

14. http://hpwren.ucsd.edu/.

15. http://www.nees.org/.

16. http://www.neoninc.org/.

17. http://www.nlanr.net/.

18. http://www.oceanleadership.org/ocean_observing.

19. http://www.rcsb.org/pdb/home/home.do.

20. http://plantsp.genomics.purdue.edu/html/.

21. http://roadnet.ucsd.edu/.

22. http://seek.ecoinformatics.org/.

23. "San Diego Supercomputer Center," 4.

24. Ibid., 6.

25. Author's presentation to the UCSD Technology Directions Committee, November 2002.

26. Ibid.

27. Ibid.

28. *Merriam-Webster's Collegiate Dictionary*, 10th ed. (2002), 704.

29. Ibid. 1150.

30. http://www.universityofcalifornia.edu/itgc/charge/welcome.html.

31. http://www.universityofcalifornia.edu/itgc/ITGC_final%20report_bw.pdf, 8.

32. http://www.universityofcalifornia.edu/itgc/supdocs/ITGC_1pg080317.pdf.

33. http://www.calit2.net/newsroom/article.php?id=307.

34. http://www.ucsd.edu/portal/site/Libraries/menuitem.346352c02aac0c82b9ba4310d34b01ca/?vgnextoid=238a2b3401904110VgnVCM10000045b410acRCRD.

35. http://www.sdsc.edu/srb/index.php/Main_Page.

36. http://masstransit.sdsc.edu/.

37. *Long-Lived Digital Data Collections Enabling Research and Education in the 21st Century*, http://www.nsf.gov/pubs/2005/nsb0540/, 9.

38. Ibid.

39. Ibid.

40. http://www.nsf.gov/pubs/2005/nsb0540/, 44.

41. "CHRONOPOLIS: Federated Digital Preservation across Time and Space," unpublished proposal (May 2004).

42. "Digital Preservation Lifecycle Management: Building a Demonstration Prototype for the Preservation of Large-Scale Multimedia Collections," unpublished proposal (March 2005).

43. "Chronopolis: Distributed Storage and Preservation Infrastructure in Support of the NDIIPP Partners Network," unpublished proposal (August 2006).

44. Francine Berman and Brian E. C. Schottlaender, "'Data' Stewardship," unpublished presentation (August 2006).

45. DataNet Program Solicitation NSF 07-601.

46. "San Diego Supercomputer Center Working Group (SDSCWG) Report," unpublished (March 2008), 1.

47. "San Diego Supercomputer Center Working Group," unpublished (March 2008), 3.

48. Ibid.

49. Francine Berman, "Next-Generation SDSC," unpublished presentation, with slight revision by the author (June 2008).

50. Phil Papadopoulos and Mike Norman, unpublished presentation (April 2008).

51. Francine Berman, personal communication to author.

52. Berman, "Next-Generation SDSC."

53. *Merriam-Webster's Collegiate Dictionary,* 23.

CHAPTER 9

THE NATIONAL AGRICULTURAL LIBRARY AND E-SCIENCE

Peter R. Young

Abstract

This chapter describes the mission, purpose, and current initiatives of the U.S. National Agricultural Library (NAL), and its collections, services, partnerships, and current digital initiatives are briefly described. In addition, the challenges and opportunities related to the development of E-research and E-science[1] that confront NAL and other research libraries are discussed and strategies to advance the role of research libraries in agricultural E-science are presented. The chapter concludes with a future NAL vision as the world's largest agricultural research library equipped to lead the conceptualization and coordinated development of new, robust global agricultural knowledge services infrastructure for the twenty-first century.

An Introduction to the National Agricultural Library

Established by the U.S. Congress in 1862 as the primary agricultural information resource of the United States, the NAL is the largest and most comprehensive agricultural library in the world. NAL is mandated by law to lead a comprehensive agricultural information network serving national and international communities.[2] NAL is engaging agricultural scientists, researchers, and others in developing the multidimensional, distributed global agricultural E-science future vision

---

The views expressed in this paper reflect those of the author and do not necessarily represent the official policies of the USDA or the NAL. In November 2008 the author assumed the position of chief of the Asian Division at the Library of Congress.

needed to enable and enhance access to all forms of agricultural information. By the authority of the establishing statute,[3] the library is assigned authority and responsibility to

- acquire, preserve, and manage information resources related to agriculture and allied sciences;
- organize agricultural information products and services, and provide them within the United States and internationally;
- plan, coordinate, and evaluate information and library needs related to agricultural research and education;
- cooperate with and coordinate efforts toward development of a comprehensive agricultural library and information network; and
- coordinate the development of specialized subject information services among the agricultural and library information communities.

NAL's Comprehensive Agricultural Information Collections

Constructed in the late 1960s, the 70 story Abraham Lincoln Building houses more than 48 miles of shelving for the library's comprehensive, multiformat collections. These total more than 2.4 million volumes of books and periodicals, and over 3.6 million documents. The library's collections reflect all aspects of agriculture and the related sciences in all formats, and include materials in more than 70 languages. Reflecting an astonishing variety of agricultural interests, NAL's collections include over 13,000 journal titles and constitute one of the largest collections of "grey" literature in agriculture in the world. In addition, these comprehensive collections contain many unique, rare, fragile, and irreplaceable items included in over 365 special collections.

NAL's processed collections contain 166,435 *unique* book and journal titles, nearly nine times the average of 19,000 in collections of members of the Association of Research Libraries (ARL).[4] Many of these items are scheduled for digital reformatting in order to ensure long-term access and preservation. The origin of NAL's collections dates to an 1839 congressional mandate to purchase books for the Agricultural Division of the Patent Office. Today, NAL provides access to an immense collection of scientific literature, books, journals, audiovisuals, reports, theses, software, laser discs, artifacts, and images related to agriculture, and to a widening array of digital media and data resources from the full spectrum of agriculture-related sciences. The library's collection contains items dating from the sixteenth century to the present, including the most complete repository of U.S. Department of Agriculture (USDA) publications, and an extensive set of materials on the history of agriculture in the United States. The collections cover all aspects of agriculture and the related sciences, and provide a comprehensive resource for agricultural scientists, policy makers, students, regulators, and scholars.

Building NAL Collections

The library has primary responsibility for collecting and retaining all publications of all 28 USDA component agencies, and is the U.S. national library with a legal mandate to collect comprehensively in the following disciplines: animal sciences, plant sciences, agricultural economics and statistics, agricultural products, agricultural chemistry and engineering, agronomy and soil conservation, forestry and forest products, rural sociology and rural life, food sciences, and nutrition. In addition to these core subjects, NAL collections contain extensive materials in related subjects such as biology, natural history, wildlife ecology, pollution, genetics, natural resources, meteorology, and fisheries.

Since the mid-1800s, NAL has carried out a global acquisitions program to secure publications through international exchange. The types of publications received on exchange are often difficult to acquire through established subscription vendors, and constitute an elusive body of grey literature not widely available from traditional sources. Currently, NAL initiates and coordinates these exchanges with over 5,000 partners from 106 countries worldwide, accounting for about 70 percent of all periodicals currently received. In general, NAL's acquisition program and collection development policies are based upon the library's responsibility to provide service to the employees of the USDA, U.S. land-grant universities,[5] and the general public in all subjects pertaining to agriculture. The NAL Collection Development Policy[6] outlines the scope of subjects collected and the degree of coverage for each subject. This policy is regularly revised to include emerging subject areas and to incorporate guidelines for collecting material in new formats, especially digital formats. NAL, the U.S. National Library of Medicine, and the Library of Congress have developed cooperative collection-development policy statements for the following subject areas: biotechnology, human nutrition and food; and veterinary sciences.

Since the mid-1990s, NAL has adjusted its acquisition and collection development procedures[7] to incorporate an increasing and growing component of digital content. This has been accompanied by expansion of the quantity of agricultural information collected and distributed in digital formats as the library transitions toward a future National Digital Library for Agriculture (NDLA).

Special Collections

The NAL special collections program emphasizes access to and preservation of rare and unique materials documenting the history of agriculture and related sciences. Items in the library's special collections include rare books, manuscripts, nursery and seed trade catalogs, posters, and photographs, plus other rare and unique materials documenting agricultural subjects. Materials date from the 1500s to the late 1900s and include many international resources. Detailed information about NAL special collections is available on the NAL Web site.[8]

Preservation

NAL is committed to the preservation of custodial collections and has greatly improved its environmental quality to extend the longevity of all materials housed in special collections. The long-term strategy is to ensure that a growing corpus of agricultural information is systematically identified, prioritized, preserved, and archived. The library has a program which has digitally reformatted a collection of USDA publications, including the *Home and Garden Bulletin*, the *Agriculture Information Bulletin*, the *Agricultural Economic Report*, and *Yearbook of the United States Department of Agriculture*. Other historical USDA publications include the *Report of the Commissioner of Agriculture*, published from 1862 to 1888, continued by the *Report of the Secretary of Agriculture*, published from 1889 to 1893. *Century of Service: The First 100 Years of the United States Department of Agriculture*, published in 1963, explores the history of the department from its establishment in 1862 by Abraham Lincoln through President John F. Kennedy's administration. NAL also has begun the digitizing of the popular *Agriculture Handbook* series, making available online access to these and other full-text publications via the NAL Digital Repository (AgSpace).

Information Access and Delivery Services

NAL's extensive 40,000 page Web site[9] generates over 90 million direct customer-service transactions annually. AGRICOLA,[10] NAL's premier index and catalog, provides open access to more than five million records. Available on the NAL Web site since 1998, AGRICOLA allows users to search and navigate the wealth of agricultural information contained in the library's comprehensive processed collections. By providing desktop Web access to a growing digital resource of scientific articles, NAL's Digital Desktop Library for USDA service (DigiTop)[11] has grown steadily in use since its inception in 2002. A total of 900,000 articles are downloaded each year by USDA scientists and researchers from this service. The DigiTop service provides 112,000 employees of the USDA, located around the world, with online access to over 14 million articles and to 64 million records in over 5,000 online journals and citation databases.

NAL is planning the implementation of a digital repository of agricultural content and large-scale scientific data sets that will support future scientific research and discovery. Working to develop this digital repository using the DSpace open-source platform, NAL has recently instituted the AgSpace digital repository. From genetic research to biotechnology to geographic-information systems to computer models and simulations, the creation of massive research data sets is generating transformational changes in the conduct of science. These changes offer opportunities for NAL to support research that enhances understanding, learning, and new scientific discovery through the development of tools and methods for organizing and using these interdisciplinary, large-scale digital data collections. NAL's planning for the agricultural E-science NDLA extends the library's historical mandate. Given the increasing complexity of agricultural research and the increasing demands of a highly network-literate public, the library is responding by developing an increasingly digital service-delivery model. This important topic is explored in more detail in a subsequent portion of this chapter devoted to agricultural E-science and NDLA development.

Networks of Cooperation

Working in partnership with U.S. land-grant universities and other agricultural information institutions worldwide, NAL provides support for the Agriculture Network Information Center (AgNIC)[12] alliance, established in 1995. AgNIC alliance members provide Web access to selected and evaluated expert information and resources covering a wide array of agricultural topics. Each AgNIC member institution has responsibility for providing and maintaining a comprehensive Web resource on a specific area of agricultural science. NAL serves as the secretariat for AgNIC's many programs and initiatives related to improving access to agricultural information resources for the nation. Using open-source software, NAL's AgNIC technical staff develops and maintains the AgNIC portal in conjunction with partner institutions. NAL supports specific cooperative agreements with AgNIC partners to digitize relevant agricultural extension and experiment-station publications included in partners' institutional collections. In 2007, the combined, annual AgNIC-partner Web statistics showed over 170 million Web hits.

AgNIC's Web portal provides access to quality agricultural information selected by AgNIC partners. AgNIC's 60-plus member institutions offer a wide array of content-rich, subject-specific Web sites. Recently, AgNIC partners adopted a new strategic plan, launched two new features—AgOAI and a news aggregator—and continued to build full-text content through a variety of projects. The AgOAI feature uses the Open Archives Initiative protocols to harvest metadata for full-text resources from targeted institutional repositories and collections in order to provide access through a single point. The news aggregator pulls news from over 20 different, reliable news sources into a central news site.

As the U.S. node of an international agricultural information system, the library also serves as a gateway for international agricultural libraries and information centers to access U.S. agricultural libraries and resources. NAL cooperates with other libraries, information centers, and consortia via several reciprocal agreements. In this regard, NAL is part of the Agricultural Libraries Network, which is a voluntary network of agricultural libraries around the world with strong regional/country coverage and other institutions with comprehensive or very specialized subject resource collections. This network is part of the United Nations information system.

AgSpace

AgSpace is the NAL's digital repository, a combination of several of NAL's digital services development and implementation initiatives. The library has undertaken several projects to digitize, store, and provide online access to historical print documents. The majority of the nearly 300,000 pages currently available online are digital versions of USDA documents. The full text of these materials and more information about these digitization projects is available from NAL's Web site.[13]

Concurrently, the library is developing and implementing procedures to collect, store, and make publicly available the current research publications of USDA scientists and employees. More than 15,000 articles had been added to the repository through the spring of 2008. NAL is working closely with USDA agencies to acquire research products that are produced at pubic expense by federal scientists in the course of their official duties. AgSpace is expected to become the first and primary provider of persistent and long-term access to all USDA publications and research products.

Long-range plans for AgSpace include collecting, maintaining, and providing access to a broad range of agricultural information in a wide variety of digital formats. The end result will be a perpetual, reliable, publicly accessible repository of digital documents, data sets, images, audiovisual files, etc., related to agriculture.

AGRICOLA

AGRICultural On-Line Access (AGRICOLA), initiated in 1970, is the catalog and index to NAL collections as well as a primary public source for worldwide access to agricultural information. All five million records in AGRICOLA are available for searching on the Web,[14] but may also be accessed on a fee basis through several commercial vendors, both online and on CD-ROM. Users may also subscribe to the AGRICOLA file on a fee basis from the National Technical Information Service, a component of the U.S. Department of Commerce. The AGRICOLA database covers materials in all formats, including printed works from the fifteenth century. The records describe publications and resources encompassing all aspects of agriculture and allied disciplines. Thousands of AGRICOLA records contain links to networked Web resources. The AGRICOLA database is organized into two components, updated with newly cataloged and indexed materials, searchable separately or together: the NAL Public Access Catalog, containing citations to books, audiovisual materials, serial titles, and other materials in the NAL collection, and the NAL Article Citation Database, which includes citations to serial articles, book chapters, reports, and reprints. AGRICOLA also contains some bibliographic records for items cataloged by other libraries but not held in NAL collections.

NAL recently "re-scoped" the AGRICOLA index by concentrating on fewer overall titles but offering more links to full-text articles. AGRICOLA now avoids covering those titles indexed by other abstracting and indexing services. To be considered for indexing in AGRICOLA, publications must meet at least one of the following criteria. They must be:

1. USDA publications or publications containing articles or chapters authored by USDA employees;
2. material related to NAL's information centers' topical areas;

3. journal articles or serial chapters on core agricultural topics, written in the English language; and

4. items that are not covered by commercial abstracting and indexing services.

The 2009 list of publications indexed in AGRICOLA may be found posted on NAL's Web site.[15] The rescoped AGRICOLA index continues to serve as the primary search tool offering access to NAL collections.

Information Management and Information Technology

Over the past quarter-century, NAL has applied digital information technology to the management of agricultural information. Technological developments spearheaded by NAL date back to the early 1950s, when NAL Director Ralph R. Shaw applied "electronic machines" to the control and retrieval of agricultural literature. These efforts included the photo-charger, rapid-selector, and photo-clerk applications based on Vannevar Bush's Memex concept. These efforts can be traced back to an article by Vannevar Bush published in 1945.[16] Bush's article proposed a Memex concept for the display and organization of information in nonlinear form. The Memex was both a library and a desk with screens to display microfilm versions of the books and articles stored in the machine's memory. NAL has continued this tradition of applying computer technology to agricultural information since then, and the library has steadily moved toward full implementation of the digital Memex vision. Over the past decade, NAL has fully implemented the Voyager integrated library system (ILS). The NAL Voyager ILS system now supports acquisition ordering, receiving, and invoice processing for purchases, and it includes modules for creating and maintaining indexing and catalog records for the AGRICOLA database as well as circulation and Online Public Access Catalog modules. In addition, NAL staff is implementing the Meridian system for management and control of electronic resources. The Voyager system has also been integrated with the Relais system in support of NAL interlibrary loan and document delivery services.

NAL is known for its expertise in developing and using a thesaurus or controlled vocabulary for organizing agricultural information collections. The NAL Agricultural Thesaurus (NALT)[17] is a hierarchical vocabulary of agricultural and biological terms. Updated annually, NALT broadly defines the subject scope of agriculture, organized according to 17 subject categories, with 2,418 definitions. Biological nomenclature comprises most terms in the thesaurus, although it includes terminology in the supporting biological, physical, and social sciences.

Originally prepared to meet the needs of the Agricultural Research Service scientists, the NALT is now extensively used to aid retrieval in agricultural information systems within USDA and elsewhere, including extension services. NALT provides an authoritative indexing vocabulary for NAL's bibliographic database of 3.75 million article citations to agricultural resources that are included in the AGRICOLA database. NAL released the sixth edition of NALT in early January 2007, adding about 400 new definitions for a total of 68,564 terms. Terminology associated with geospatial technology, agricultural economics, tropical trees, and fire science was expanded in this latest edition. The taxonomic classification of fish was reviewed and updated according to nomenclature approved by the American Fisheries Society. The NAL Glossary provides a collection of definitions for agricultural terms developed in conjunction with the creation of the NALT. The 2007 edition contains over 2,400 terms ranging across agriculture and its many ancillary subjects, most composed and defined by the NAL Thesaurus Staff.

NALT-*ESPAÑOL*

In May 2007, NAL published Spanish language versions of its NALT and Glossary of Agricultural Terms. The NALT and Glossary in Spanish support increased Spanish language access to agricultural information throughout the United States and the world, accommodating the complexity of the Spanish language from a Western Hemisphere perspective. This first Spanish-language edition of NALT has more than 15,700 translated concepts, and contains definitions for more than 2,400 concepts in both English and Spanish, which are also published in a separate interface as the Glossary of Agricultural Terms. Both language versions of these publications can be accessed through the NAL Services Web page.[18]

Publishing a Spanish language edition of the NALT makes the thesaurus a valuable bilingual reference tool useful to speakers of both the Spanish and English languages. Organizations using NALT terms can easily add a Spanish language capability to their agricultural information applications. Of the estimated 480 million Spanish-speaking people in the world, about 87 percent live in the Western Hemisphere. Spanish is the second most widely spoken language in the United States, and is the most rapidly growing language used in U.S. agriculture. Future Spanish-language editions of the NALT will change in response to recommendations from the Spanish-speaking agricultural community and NAL cooperators. Translation of the NALT into Spanish was accomplished by NAL with the American Distance Education Consortium (ADEC). ADEC is a nonprofit, international distance-education consortium of approximately 65 state universities and land-grant colleges. ADEC promotes the creation and provision of high-quality, economical distance-education programs and services for diverse audiences.

NAL Information Centers

Operating within NAL's overall program structure, the library's information centers are reliable sources of science-based information in key areas of American agriculture. By collaborating with other organizations throughout government, the centers provide timely, accurate, comprehensive, and in-depth coverage in their specialized subject areas. Staffs of these information centers make specialized information available through the NAL Web site, and help library users find answers to specific questions and begin more extensive research programs. Each of NAL's information centers has its own Web site and is a partner in the AgNIC. NAL maintains eight information centers:

- The Alternative Farming Systems Information Center (AFSIC)[19]
- The Animal Welfare Information Center (AWIC)[20]
- The Food and Nutrition Information Center (FNIC)[21]
- The Food Safety Information Center (FSIC)[22]
- The National Invasive Species Information Center (NISIC)[23]
- The Rural Information Center[24]
- The Technology Transfer Information Center[25]
- The Water Quality Information Center(WQIC)[26]

Web-Based Products and Services

NAL continues to expand its presence on the World Wide Web to provide access to information for its global clientele on an every-hour-of-every-day basis.
In 2007, the NAL Web site

- received an average of more than seven million "hits" each month from people seeking agricultural information; NAL anticipates that Web site usage will increase in response to the site's user-friendly design, enhanced searching capabilities, and continual improvement in content;
- incorporated Distributed eXPLORIT to its entire Web site to facilitate comprehensive unified search; and
- achieved an American Customer Services Index score of 71 points, an improvement of five points above the 2006 level.

In early October 2007, the library began its first blog—InfoFarm: The NAL Blog[27]—becoming the 16th active U.S. federal government Web log. The purpose of InfoFarm is to give NAL a human, personal voice on issues related to agriculture and agricultural information; give NAL customers a fresh glimpse of NAL's services and resources; and give NAL a chance to interact with customers. The Special Libraries Association wrote, "InfoFarm is written in an engaging style with lots of links to great websites and is certain to interest anyone who eats food. Thanks, NAL!"

Nutrition.gov

In collaboration with other USDA agencies, NAL operates the Nutrition.gov[28] Web site, providing vetted, science-based nutrition information for the general consumer-public. This popular site highlights the latest in nutrition news and tools from across U.S. government agencies. A team of dietitians and nutrition information specialists at NAL's Food and Nutrition Information Center maintain Nutrition.gov and provide reference services to answer customer questions on food and nutrition issues. Nutrition.gov is an important resource for developing food- and exercise-based strategies related to weight management, and for disseminating the work of multiple U.S. federal agencies in a national obesity-prevention effort. Nutrition.gov includes databases, recipes, interactive tools, and specialized information for infants and children, adult men and women, and seniors. The site links to information on the USDA food pyramid, dietary guidelines, dietary supplements, fitness, and food safety. In 2007, Nutrition.gov averaged more than 350,000 hits per month and was ranked number one by the Google search engine as a source of information on human nutrition. In order of popularity, the top three subjects on which visitors sought more information were "Smart Nutrition 101," weight management, and food composition.

The National Digital Library for Agriculture Vision

NAL has initiated planning for the collaborative development of a NDLA, which, by extension, will provide a vision and conceptual model for development of a Global Research Library for Agriculture to support E-science in agriculture. At one level, the vision of NDLA responds to the need for end-to-end agricultural data management, from data acquisition, sharing, integration, and management to data treatment, provenance identification, and persistence in the agricultural, natural, and life sciences. At a more global level, the NDLA vision addresses the changing dynamics associated with agricultural knowledge creation and data use in E-science, which can have a profound effect on the ability of science to develop solutions in response to a range of challenges involving global health, environmental concerns, and food safety and supply. Data constitute the glue needed to achieve collaborative agricultural research. Sharing of research data among scientists provides a mechanism to leverage network technology in support of the research process. The role of the research library in this process is critical for the success of E-science.

NDLA agricultural E-science collaboration requires multi-institutional, cross-sector, multidisciplinary, global, and open access to a wide array of content, data, and services, available through a shared, interoperable network. Such an NDLA E-science vision is intended to encourage innovative changes in the conduct of research related to the agricultural sciences, and to capitalize on the potential of global digital networks to transform engagement, discovery, and learning in education, research, and knowledge creation. The implementation of a new generation of digital systems, tools, and services is necessary to facilitate the organization, management, curation, preservation, and delivery of massive quantities of scientific data being generated by research for the benefit of scientists, producers, students, and practitioners.

Future scientific research and learning require an information-content infrastructure capable of delivering the appropriate services, tools, and capabilities needed to integrate digital information and data into the fabric of scientific research-and-discovery processes in an interdisciplinary environment. Such capabilities are especially appropriate for the biological (animal and plant), chemical, natural, and environmental sciences, for engineering, and for those social sciences related to agriculture, such as agricultural economics. These domains share large data access, capture, storage, description, integration, and manipulation requirements for domains such as animal and plant genomics, genetic sequencing, functional genomics, proteomics, metabolomics, synthetic biology, watersheds, biofuel and renewable energy, aquaculture, land and water usage, and geographic information. These fields are increasingly dependent upon the ability of multidisciplinary teams to share and employ digital data collected from multiple sources. The challenges of establishing interoperable systems, syntax, semantics, and standards across multiple platforms, applications, and formats are not insignificant. This deluge of scientific data is often inherently messy, unstructured, and lacking in standards. The variability of scientific data means that it is malleable, mobile, and mutable. Data can present challenges well beyond the familiar structures, processes, and operations involving documents and published article content.

Given the complex nature of data-intensive research, no single library or research institution can be expected to acquire, manage, and preserve the growing range of digital data and knowledge content related to the multidisciplinary domains of agriculture. Knowledge discovery and research productivity in the agricultural sciences will increasingly require access to the comprehensive array of resources, services, and tools that only an NDLA could provide.

The following points relate to the development of agricultural E-science:

- E-science plays a critical role in accelerating key breakthroughs in science including the discovery of new knowledge needed to protect the earth's life-support systems, on which life depends for survival.
- A growing awareness of a "gathering storm" of threats to human health, food safety, the environment, and the availability of land and water resources for human, industrial, and agricultural uses requires attention to issues of scientific communication, content access, and services essential to scholarship and scientific discovery.
- Access to a full range of scientific and scholarly publications, data resources, and related services are fundamental for education and learning, as well as for educated consumers.
- Global competitiveness requires that knowledge institutions develop new methods and arrangements for continual long-term access to scientific and research knowledge content.
- The U.S. National Institutes of Health has made significant progress in developing global systems and tools for the human health sciences in the biomedical, molecular biology, and biochemistry fields. However, future research in the agricultural sciences will require a scalable and technologically advanced information and data infrastructure sufficient to address the growing demands of agricultural research and the life sciences, especially as the demands relate to genomic sequence data and functional genomics information, as applied to the full range of plants, animals, and microbes.

Concepts and general requirements for agricultural E-science implementation require content components and partnership relationships to enable NAL and the research library community to address the increasing demand for agriculture-related information from scientists, researchers, growers, students, industry producers, and the general public. The following basic E-science requirements and components are fundamental:

- development and coordination of institutional, disciplinary, domain, and national federated digital repositories for the agricultural disciplines;
- network access to evaluated content resources from noncommercial Web sources;
- integrated network access to commercially published agricultural content literature in digital form;
- digital reformatting of printed content;
- digital data content capture and preservation;
- curatorial and preservation services for visualization, simulation, synthesis, analysis, manipulation, discovery, and presentation of digital data resources related to agriculture;
- the development of cyberinfrastructure, grid-computing, platform-system environments and services required to deal effectively with networked agricultural scientific data resources.

NAL's plans for developing the NDLA for agricultural E-science build on NAL's historic leadership in the application of information technology to facilitate access and delivery of relevant content in support of agriculture. By developing the AGRICOLA database, creating the Agricultural Network Information Center alliance, and introducing the USDA Digital Desktop Library service and the AgSpace digital repository, NAL has achieved significant success in the application of digital information technology to the provision of agricultural information and related services.

The NDLA concept is consistent with NAL's leadership in the formation of AgNIC which involves more than 60 institutions working in partnership to facilitate access to quality information resources related to all aspects of agriculture, food, and natural resources. Since the AgNIC alliance was established, its members' work has evolved through several generations of network technology. The members have established metadata and vocabulary standards, and have recently implemented portal and Web services applications, including an OAI harvester, serving the agricultural community. The cooperation and partnership inherent in the AgNIC alliance model are essential to the development of the NDLA concept and vision.

Such an integrated but multifaceted NDLA vision can only be successfully launched and sustained through close partnership relations with a host of institutions on a global scale. The policy and administrative challenges are no less formidable than the technological issues. But the enormity of the challenges pales in comparison with the potential advancements. To be effective this NDLA agricultural E-science concept requires a global context reflecting the global nature of agricultural science issues and the significant global challenges in these fields.

Recent Trends in Information and Knowledge Use

Recent relevant trends include the following:

- "Search and seize" information-seeking activities predominate, especially among younger students.
- Migration is occurring from printed documents to electronic content.
- Demand is increasing for grey literature, data, and analytical tools.
- Priority is shifting from back-room processing efficiencies to effective end-user satisfaction.
- A shift is occurring to targeted, customized, market-subsegment audience services.
- Customers are working from field laboratories, the bench, and home, demanding mobile and global service availability.
- The rapid shift from ownership to access is changing the research library mission from one of collecting the world's knowledge base to a more open access arrangement through partnerships.
- Concern for both access and assets reflects a growing focus on data preservation.
- The need is increasing for links to digital from print content.
- User/patron/customer needs and requirements are increasingly diverse.
- Image/text/data format integration is occurring.
- The need is increasing for research findings to relate to the general public.

The blend of these trends in information and knowledge services, along with emerging trends in agriculture and agricultural science research heighten attention to agricultural issues and to the need for agricultural research to address global challenges. These trends are also creating a realization that a new generation of tools is needed to support E-science research processes related to agriculture. In response to knowledge-service trends over the past decade, research libraries have incorporated new content, new technologies, and new network services to meet increased user expectations. The NDLA concept vision is consistent with the principles of E-science and is presented in response to these changes in an attempt to take advantage of a host of emerging opportunities and to address significant challenges in the field of agriculture.

The NDLA concept is an extension of a distributed digital library model. The concept incorporates network-connected digital content repositories that are linked to provide a range of access and services to meet a wide spectrum of scientific and research requirements. The conceptual framework for the NDLA incorporates collaborative relations with institutional partners to focus on the coordinated digital reformatting and preservation of printed U.S. agricultural documents and publications (including USDA publications, the host of U.S. extension-service publications, and related grey literature resources in the agricultural-related disciplines), the digital capture and preservation of Web resources related to the agricultural sciences, and the development of distributed network technology infrastructure required to maintain and preserve agricultural research data and tools for manipulation, analysis, visualization, and presentation. In short, such a multifaceted NDLA vision (preserving printed publications, capture of digital Web objects and content, and deployment of research data repositories) could only be successful through close partnership relations with a host of institutions. Each essential component is reviewed below.

Linked Access to Noncommercial Web Content

Web access links to evaluated digital content resources from noncommercial research sources is needed to support agricultural E-science. NDLA network access to such resources builds on the current AgNIC Alliance model. AgNIC alliance partners, including NAL's information centers, establish links to relevant subject content. Evaluation, selection, capture, integration, and preservation of relevant Web content provide the basis for establishing and maintaining links through a customizable interface. Access is provided through cross-database, federated search engines and discovery tools. Such a decentralized model for global access is the basis for the Food and Agriculture (FAO United Nations) portal for an animal health and plant disease site that is currently under development. The use of thesaurus tools and controlled vocabulary in conjunction with Web content linking ensures logical and relevant search results for linked access to noncommercial Web content.

Linked Access to Commercial Web Content

Web access links to evaluated digital content resources from commercial sources form an additional component of the NDLA concept for E-science agriculture. This concept is the basis for NAL's USDA DigiTop service by which the 110,000-plus employees of the USDA have online 24/7/365 access to digital content articles in current and retrospective professional and scientific journals, along with services from a host of related digital database services in the agricultural sciences. The USDA DigiTop service is offered by NAL through subscription licenses with over sixty commercial scientific and professional publishers. From an initial pilot feasibility project in 2002 and 2003, NAL now offers this service on a programmatic basis for all USDA workers regardless of location throughout the United States and in locations around the world.

Digital Reformatting for Preservation of Print Repositories

Digital preservation formatting for print content is another component of the NDLA concept for E-science agriculture. Development of structures for capturing and preserving of digitally reformatted printed content requires standards development and implementation through a nationally coordinated program by which digital scanning, preservation reformatting, and metadata standards are developed. In the agricultural sciences especially, grey-literature capture and reformatting is a critical area for concentration. Over the last decade, NAL has fostered such digital reformatting collaboration among AgNIC partner institutions and other U.S. land-grant universities in a coordinated program funded through the National Endowment for the Humanities.

Cyberinfrastructure for Digital Agricultural E-Science

Recent advances in information technologies and communication systems have the potential to redefine the nature and conduct of scientific research. This concept of involving research libraries in the development of E-science was explored by a Joint Task Force on Library Support for E-Science of the ARL. The task force report—*Agenda for Developing E-Science in Research Libraries: Final Report and Recommendations to the Scholarly Communication Steering Committee, the Public Policies Affecting Research Libraries Steering Committee, and the Research, Teaching, and Learning Steering Committee* (November 2007)—is available from ARL.[29] Increasingly, agricultural scientific research activities posit the need for development of a cyberinfrastructure consisting of high-performance computational resources, massive data-storage repositories, next-generation networks, digital library databases, application frameworks, and E-science tools. Such a shared cyberinfrastructure is needed to support scientists and researchers engaged in team-based research. Not clearly defined are the roles, capacities, and capabilities of research libraries to lead in the development of E-science repositories and systems. As the ARL's task force report reflects, "Clearly e-science has the potential to be transformational within research libraries by impacting their operations, functions, and possibly even mission."

Developments in digital and network technologies offer opportunities for NAL to collaboratively develop NDLA E-science agriculture services for researchers. Such services would employ high-speed, broadband digital networks. They would include data acquisition, repository, preservation, and curatorial services. And they would provide tools to facilitate data manipulation, exploration, synthesis, analysis, simulation, visualization, and discovery. Such an effort would support global scientific collaboration in such areas as functional genomics, proteomics, and metabolomics, as well as enabling simulation/modeling applications for environmental/ecological studies. These emerging interdisciplinary fields require high-capacity mass-storage systems, large-scale archival data repositories, and cyberinfrastructure networking technologies. NDLA plans to develop these research data services to complement NAL's information management and delivery services for USDA and other scientists. Included are Web information services, federated searching functionality, clustering engines, and the development of a comprehensive Agricultural Science Researcher Portal, which would provide integrated access to scientific articles and research publication content, as well as research data archives and the means to use these resources effectively.

As an example of the nature of E-research in the agricultural sciences, the potential for synthetic biology for rewiring the genetic circuitry of living organisms offers some idea of how NAL can respond to the data-driven science challenge and opportunity.[30] Scientists in the field of synthetic biology are working to modify microbes to generate cheap petroleum out of plant waste by creating DNA segments, some over 580,000 units long, to be used in the creation of synthetic cells that are needed for further research. Sophisticated and complex procedures promise a better under-standing of biological systems through the construction of synthetic systems. This research also employs new technology developed for genome sequencing.[31] These complex systems require instrumentation to capture, analyze, manage, and store several terabytes of data generated per day—an unprecedented amount of data to capture, manage, and preserve. It is expected that this research will necessitate an increase to petabyte- and exabyte-scale systems in the near future.

Computational biology presents but one of a growing number of agricultural research-related initiatives that require new, large-scale data capabilities. The require-ments are giving new meaning to the "data processing" issues that dominated the early days of digital computing nearly five decades ago. In a very real sense, these large-scale data-processing requirements are prompting a reconceptualization of the basic assumptions of networking. The development of an NDLA component for E-science agricultural cyberinfrastructure results from recent advances in computa-tional biology and other domains in the life sciences that require large-scale distrib-uted repositories and grid-computing functionality. Such data-driven science requires an agricultural E-science infrastructure to address the need for distributed access to a growing body of scientific data, as well as the development of tools for analysis, manipulation, preservation, and repurposing of large-scale data sets. Essen-tially, enhanced data and system applications, capabilities, and efficiencies are required to create team-based digital science co-laboratories using community gate-ways or portals for collaborative knowledge development. This new information environment requires supercomputer simulations of complex systems. Computa-tional models will need to handle an unimaginable volume of data from smart sensor arrays and networks. Data validation and metadata standards are required, as are stewardship and curatorial services for enormous collections of scientific data. The enormity of the computing network and large-scale data-processing challenges to achieve E-science in agriculture is matched by challenges in other areas as well. The variant and different communication systems and cultures common to specific scientific disciplines, as well as the lack of common data notation, format, and plat-form standardization, combine to present complex and complicated hurdles to effec-tive E-science research. The interdisciplinary nature of agricultural research adds an additional layer of complexity to the multidisciplinary nature of agricultural E-science.

Despite these challenges, a global cyberinfrastructure system in support of agricul-tural E-science and research is essential to provide a platform for routine, effective, and distance-independent activities of agricultural knowledge research communities. Such virtual communities are the only method by which to address the increasingly global challenges presented by emerging diseases, food safety, and environmental degradation. In the future, world-scale collaborative teams will need to employ a cyberinfrastructure supporting E-science that offers new options for what is done, how it is done, and who participates collectively. NAL is incorporating this concept in the library's vision for the future. The global library community has the opportunity and responsibility to move from concept to collective implementation.

An NDLA for agricultural E-science is an essential component for creation of a trusted, open environment for knowledge access and creation. This NDLA program will support more extensive collaborations that will reduce research disparities, enhance research productivity, and address global challenges. The NDLA as a national and, by extension, a global, large-scale data and information infrastructure is needed to assure continued advancement in the agricultural sciences for the future. The NDLA is needed to foster community and collaboration. It is essential to foster the pursuit of knowledge by providing a space for intellectual exchange, research, learning, discovery, and innovation.

Notes

NB: Internet addresses in the following notes were accurate as of February 3, 2009.

1. E-science refers to computationally intensive science that is carried out in highly distributed network environments involving digital technologies that enable distributed collaboration.
2. NAL organic statute: P.L. 101-624, November 28, 1990.
3. 7 United States Code § 3125a.
4. Constance Malpas, "Measuring Uniqueness in System-wide Book Holdings: Implications for Collection Management," American Library Association 2008 Midwinter Meeting, Philadelphia, PA, January 12, 2008.
5. U.S. land-grant institutions are the 215 universities and colleges that are members of the National Association of State University and Land-Grant Colleges (NASULGC).
6. http://www.nal.usda.gov/about/policy/coll_dev_toc.shtml.
7. http://www.nal.usda.gov/speccoll/collect/history.html.
8. http://www.nal.usda.gov/speccoll/.
9. http://www.nal.usda.gov.
10. http://agricola.nal.usda.gov.
11. http://www.nal.usda.gov/digitop.
12. http://www.agnic.org.
13. http://nal.usda.gov/.
14. http://agricola.nal.usda.gov/.
15. http://nal.usda.gov/catalog/.
16. Vannevar Bush, "As We May Think," *Atlantic Monthly* 176, no. 1 (1945): 101–8.
17. http://agclass.nal.usda.gov/agt/agt.shtml.
18. http://www.nal.usda.gov/services/.
19. http://afsic.nal.usda.gov.
20. http://awic.nal.usda.gov.
21. http://fnic.nal.usda.gov/.
22. http://foodsafety.nal.usda.gov.
23. http://www.invasivespeciesinfo.gov.
24. http://ric.nal.usda.gov.
25. http://nal.usda.gov.
26. http://www.nal.usda.gov/wqic/.

27. http://weblogs.nal.usda.gov/infofarm/.

28. http://www.nutrition.gov.

29. http://www.arl.org/bm~doc/ARL_EScience_final.pdf.

30. Nicholas Wade, "Genetic Engineers Who Don't Just Tinker," *New York Times* (July 8, 2007): "Week in Review," 5.

31. Bernadette Toner, "Data Déjà Vu: Genome Centers Tackle IT Challenges of Next-Gen Sequencing," *GenomeWeb Daily News* (May 4, 2007), http://www.genomeweb.com/informatics/data-d%C3%A9j%C3%A0-vu-genome-centers-tackle-it-challenges-next-gen-sequencing.

INDEX

AAS. *See* American Astronomical Society

ACLS. *See* American Council of Learned Societies

ACT. *See* Administrative Computing and Telecommunications, at UCSD

Adaptive Web, 12–13

ADEC. *See* American Distance Education Consortium

Administrative Computing and Telecommunications (ACT), at UCSD, 109

AFCS. *See* Alliance for Cell Signaling

AFSIC. *See* Alternative Farming Systems Information Center

Agenda for Developing E-Science in Research Libraries: Final Report and Recommendations (ARL), 127. *See also* Association of Research Libraries, task forces and reports

AGLINET. *See* Agricultural Libraries Network

AgNIC. *See* Agriculture Network Information Center

AgOIA database, 117

AGRICOLA. *See* AGRICultural On-Line Access index and catalog

Agricultural Libraries Network (AGLINET), 117

AGRICultural On-Line Access (AGRICOLA) index and catalog, 116, 118–19, 124

Agricultural Science Researcher Portal, 127

Agriculture Network Information Center (AgNIC), 117, 121, 124, 126

AgSpace digital repository, 116–18, 124

Alliance for Cell Signaling (AFCS), 101

Alternative Farming Systems Information Center (AFSIC), 121

American Astronomical Society (AAS), 96

American Council of Learned Societies (ACLS), 71, 73, 78

American Distance Education Consortium (ADEC), 120

American Fisheries Society, 120

American Library Association, 36

Andrew W. Mellon Foundation, 87, 96

Animal Welfare Information Center (AWIC), 121

Application program interfaces, 46–47, 55, 82

Arabidopsis Information Resource, The (TAIR), 38–39

ARCHER project, 56

Archives and archival science, definition and roles, 36–37, 81

ARL. *See* Association of Research Libraries
Arms, William Y., 46
ARROW project, 56
Article Citation Database (of NAL), 118
arXiv (at Cornell University), 10
Association of Research Libraries (ARL):
    mission of, 23; task forces and reports,
    23–25, 29, 35, 44, 49–50, 56, 71, 79,
    127
Astronomy, 34, 79, 93–97, 127. *See also*
    Cosmic Genome Project; Galaxy Zoo;
    Large Synoptic Survey Telescope; Sky
    Server Web site; Sloan Digital Sky Survey
Atkins, Daniel, 73
ATLAS experiment, 80
AWIC. *See* Animal Welfare Information
    Center

Berghel, Hal, 18–19
Berlin Declaration on Open Access to
    Knowledge in the Sciences and
    Humanities, 8
Berman, Francine, 99, 102–3, 110
Bindley Bioscience Center for Genomic
    Research and Technology, 38
Bioinformatics, 4, 68, 69
Biomedical Informatics Research Network,
    101
Blue Ribbon Advisory Panel on
    Cyberinfrastructure (of NSF), 19
Blue Ribbon Task Force on Sustainable
    Digital Preservation and Access (of
    NSF), 85–86
British Library, 65
Bush, Vannevar, 119

CAIDA. *See* Cooperative Association for
    Internet Data Analysis
California Digital Library (CDL), 105
California Institute of Information
    Technology and Telecommunications
    (Calit2), 102, 108–9
Calit2. *See* California Institute of
    Information Technology and
    Telecommunications
Campus Cyberinfrastructure Working
    Group, 71

Canada Institute for Scientific and
    Technical Information (CISTI), 70
Canadian Institutes of Health Research
    (CIHR), 55
Canadian National Committee for
    CODATA, 70
CANARIE, Canada's Advanced Research
    and Innovation Network, 70
CAnet4 network (in Canada), 70
CDL. *See* California Digital Library
Center for Library Initiatives (of CIC),
    50
CERN. *See* European Organization for
    Nuclear Research
Chronopolis digital preservation program,
    106
CIC. *See* Committee on Institutional
    Cooperation
CIDT. *See* Computer Information Design
    Team, at UCSD
CIHR. *See* Canadian Institutes of Health
    Research
CISTI. *See* Canada Institute for Scientific
    and Technical Information
Climate modeling, 5
Clinical and Translational Science Awards
    program (CTSA), 53–54
CLIR. *See* Council on Library and
    Information Resources
Cloud computing, 82
CLR. *See* Council on Library Resources
CNI. *See* Coalition for Networked
    Information
Coalition for Networked Information
    (CNI), 63, 67; description of, 64;
    E-science interests of, 25, 70–73; Exec-
    utive Roundtables, 72
CODATA. *See* Canadian National
    Committee for CODATA
Collaboration and collaboratives, 73,
    104, 122, 128–29; ARL task force
    recommends, 45; examples of, 12, 27,
    50, 52, 55, 105, 117; fields required for,
    36; need for, 8–9, 21, 29–30, 66, 69, 79;
    opportunities for, 11–12, 34, 54
Collections: cause change, 5; CLIR seeks,
    85; collections of NAL, 114–15;

evolution of, 88; "hidden" collections, 87–88. *See also* Data collections

Colon Classification scheme, 36

Commission on Cyberinfrastructure in the Humanities and Social Sciences (of ACLS), 93

Commission on Preservation and Access, 84

Committee on Institutional Cooperation (CIC), 50

Computational limits, 46

Computational science, 4, 5, 128

Computer Information Design Team (CIDT), at UCSD, 109

Conference on Librarians and E-science (of CIC), 50

Congress of the United States, 71, 113

Cooperative Association for Internet Data Analysis, 101

Cornell University, 10, 46, 50, 63

Cosmic Genome Project, 94

Council on Library and Information Resources (CLIR), 64, 77, 82, 84–89

Council on Library Resources (CLR), 84

Crane, Gregory, 86

Creating a UC Cyberinfrastructure, report, 104

CTSA. *See* Clinical and Translational Science Awards program

Cyberinfrastructure: agendas for and examples of, 66, 84; assembled at UCSD, 101; changes in, 101; definition, description, and development of, 4, 63–64, 98–100; for science and E-science, 78–81, 99–100, 127–28; at SDSC, 109–10; strategies for development of, 30, 46, 66, 104

Cyberinfrastructure Report Task Force (of ACLS), 71

Cyberinfrastructure Vision for 21st Century Discovery (NSF), document, 20

Cyberscholarship, 46

DAMS. *See* Digital Asset Management System

DART project, 56

Data: access to, 6, 46, 68, 83, 116, 126; archives of, 10; authentication of, 66; authors of, 35; categories of, 25, 96; challenges of, 25–26, 34–35; definition of, 81, 106; facilities for, 72; funding for, 11, 66, 71; growth and size of, 5, 34–35, 63, 83, 128; importance of, 5, 6, 103, 106; needs for, 6, 65; policies and principles governing data, 20, 27, 68; processing of, 38; restrictions on, 79, 83–84; tools and taxonomies for, 66; transfer of, 105–6

Databases and data sets, 11, 38

Data collections, 5, 25–27, 84, 97, 116. *See also* Digital libraries

Data curation, 35, 96–97. *See also* Data management

Data issues, 49, 70

Data management: in agricultural E-science, 128; challenges faced by, 5–6, 9, 25; Chronopolis system for, 106–7; distinguished from data stewardship, 103; efficiency needed in, 68, 83; guiding principles for, 6–7; leadership needed, 6; at NAL, 119–20; problems of, 86; requirements for, 46; roles and responsibilities in, 35–38; workflow in, 10. *See also* Data curation

DataNet (of NSF). *See* Sustainable Digital Data Preservation and Access Network

Data preservation. *See* Preservation

Data repositories, 6, 10–11, 13, 27, 66, 69, 88; institutional repository movement, 96; needed for E-science, 103

Data scientists, 9, 35

DataStar supercomputer, 101

Data stewardship, 72, 103. *See also* Data management

Data Trust Alliance, 108

Data Working Group of Cornell University Library, 50

dbGaP database, 55

DCC. *See* Digital Curation Centre in the UK

Declerck, Luc, 99 n

Defense Advanced Research Projects Agency, 21

De Roure, David, 68

Developing the UK's e-Infrastructure for Science and Innovation (National e-Science Centre), report, 65

Dewey Decimal System, 36

DigArch (Digital Archiving), 107

Digital Asset Management System (DAMS), 105

Digital Curation Centre (DCC) in the UK, 56, 67, 71

Digital Desktop Library (DigiTop), 116, 126

Digital libraries: development of, 21–23, 28; and E-science, 10, 12; infrastructure, 21–23; of NAL, 116–17. *See also* Data collections

Digital Library Federation (DLF), 22, 64

Digital Library Infrastructure on Grid Enabled Technology (DILIGENT), 56

Digital Preservation Repository of the California Digital Library, 105–6

Digital Research and Curation Center (DRCC), 95, 96, 97

Digital scholarship, 36, 84

DigiTop. *See* Digital Desktop Library

DiLauro, Tim, 93 n

DILIGENT. *See* Digital Library Infrastructure on Grid Enabled Technology

DLF. *See* Digital Library Federation

DRCC. *See* Digital Research and Curation Center

DSpace digital repository, 116

Dynes, Robert, 102

Earth System Initiative (at MIT), 49

Earth systems, 5

Ecology, 78

Education and training, 11, 20, 66, 77

EDUCAUSE, 64, 71

E-infrastructure, 63–64. *See also* Cyberinfrastructure

Ellis, Art, 108

Emory University, 51

Entrez search-engine system, 46, 55

Epidemiology, 84

E-repositories. *See* Data repositories

E-science: in agriculture, 123–24; building

understanding of, 6, 23–25; in Canada, 70; challenges to, 110; changes in, 5, 78; definition, description, methodology, and origins of, 4, 13, 19, 24, 34, 43, 63–64, 79, 129 n.1; effects of, 48, 82; in European Union, 69–70; hybrid structures needed for, 7; at Johns Hopkins University, 93–97; and libraries, 17, 26, 30, 33–34, 44–46, 71, 81–84; at NAL, 113–29; policies for, 44; relationship to cyberinfrastructure, 4, 79, 80, 99–100, 127; reports on, 19–20, 24–25, 67, 69; strategies for, 74; tools needed for, 5–6; trends in, 3–4, 5, 18–20, 24; in United Kingdom, 34, 65–69; at University of California, San Diego, 99–110

E-science Task Force of the Association of Research Libraries, 18, 23–25, 29. *See also* Joint Task Force on Library Support for E-Science

European Organization for Nuclear Research (CERN), 4, 80, 81

European Research Area, 69

eXPLORIT (in NAL), 121

FAO. *See* Food and Agriculture portal of the United Nations

FAPESP, State of São Paulo Research Foundation in Brazil, 80, 81

Fedora repository software, 96

FITS. *See* Flexible Image Transport System

Flexible Image Transport System (FITS), 94

FNIC. *See* Food and Nutrition Information Center

Food and Agriculture portal of the United Nations (FAO), 126

Food and Nutrition Information Center (FNIC), 121

Food Safety Information Center (FSIC), 121

Fox, Marye Anne, 103

Frye Institute, 22

FSIC. *See* Food Safety Information Center

Galaxy Zoo, 94

General Atomics, 100
Genomics, 13, 80, 123
GEON. *See* Geosciences Network
Geosciences Network (GEON), 101
Global Research Library 2020, 54
Google, 7, 48, 122
Greenstein, Dan, 22
Greer, Christopher, 36, 79
Grid computing, 100
Grid Operations Support Centre (in UK), 67

Hanisch, Bob, 93 n
Harte-Hanks marketing company, 86
HEFCE. *See* Higher Education Funding Council of England
Henry, Charles, 84
Hey, Tony and Jessie, 6, 43, 54, 65
"Hidden" collections, 87–88
Higher Education Funding Council of England (HEFCE), 66
High-performance computing, 20, 46
High Performance Wireless Research and Education Network (HPWREN), 101
HPWREN. *See* High Performance Wireless Research and Education Network
Humanities, 85
Hume, Wyatt R. (Rory), 103
Hunter, Jane, 27

IBM Blue Gene eServer, 101
I-Center pentagram, 36–37
ICPSR. *See* Interuniversity Consortium for Social and Political Research
IDC market intelligence firm, 83
IDIES. *See* Institute for Data Intensive Engineering and Science
InfoFarm: The NAL Blog, 121
Informatics and information specialists, 6, 11, 29, 74
Information. *See* Data
Information technology, 78, 103–4, 119–20
Information Technology Guidance Committee (at University of California), 103–4
Information Technology Leadership

Council (at University of California), 104
Infrastructure development, 95. *See also* Cyberinfrastructure
Institute for Data Intensive Engineering and Science (IDIES), 93–94
Institute of Museum and Library Services, 21, 28–29, 85, 93 n, 96
Institute of Translational Health Sciences, 54
International Journal of Digital Libraries, 12
International Virtual Observatory Alliance (IVOA), 94
Internet, 5, 70, 7177, 99
Interoperability, 72
Interuniversity Consortium for Social and Political Research (ICPSR), 108
Ionomics Information Management System, 39
IVOA. *See* International Virtual Observatory Alliance

JISC. *See* Joint Information Systems Committee
Johns Hopkins University, 12, 51, 93–97. *See also* Sheridan Libraries
Joint Information Systems Committee (JISC), 55, 64–68, 71, 85
Joint Task Force on Library Support for E-science, 44–47, 49–50, 56; members of, 59; recommendations of, 59–60, 127. *See also* E-science Task Force of the Association of Research Libraries

Karin, Sid, 102
Karst Collaborative Workspace, University of New Mexico, 12

Large Hadron Collider, 4, 80
Large Synoptic Survey Telescope, 5, 34–35, 38
Leadership, 6, 84
LEAD project. *See* Linked Environments for Atmospheric Discovery
Learning Spaces Program (of CNI), 72
Librarians: involvement in scholarly communication changes, 28–29; roles

and opportunities, 28–30, 34–38, 41, 74, 84; skills needed, 6, 28–30, 46

Libraries: challenges to, 82; and E-science, 30, 33–34, 41, 44–47, 51, 56, 81–84; new structures for, 7–8; opportunities for, 8–10, 34; organization of, 35–36, 51–53, 84; roles of, 7, 9, 13, 20, 22, 25–27, 30, 35–38, 41, 54, 81–84, 122. *See also by individual names*

Library Association in Britain, 36

Library of Congress, 36, 55, 71, 85, 96, 102, 107, 113 n, 115

Library science, 36–37, 93

Library Support for E-Science Task Force (of ARL), 71

LIFE. *See* Life Cycle Information for E-Literature

Life Cycle Information for E-Literature, 86

Life Under Your Feet soil-ecology resource, 95

Linked Environments for Atmospheric Discovery (LEAD), 20

Literacy, changes in, 78

Long-Lived Digital Data Collections, Enabling Research and Education in the 21st Century (National Science Board), report, 25, 34–35

Los Alamos National Laboratory Research Library, 12

Lynch, Clifford, 28, 63 n, 73

Massachusetts Institute of Technology (MIT), 49

Mass Transit project of CDL and SDSC, 105

Memex, 119

Meridian system, 119

Metabolomics, 123

Metadata, 6, 66, 72, 97, 103, 105

Microsoft Corporation, 54, 65, 93 n, 96

"Million books problem," 86

Mitchell, Maria, 79

Molecular biology, 55

Museums, 81

NAL. *See* National Agricultural Library

NALT. *See* National Agricultural Library Thesaurus

NALT-*ESPAÑOL*, 120

nanoHUB, 39–41

Nanotechnology, 39–41

National Academy of Sciences, 34, 71

National Aeronautics and Space Administration, 21

National Agricultural Library (NAL), 55; Article Citation Database, 118; collections of, 114–15; description and history of, 113–14; and E-science, 113–29; information centers and services of, 120–21; preservation in, 116; Public Access Catalog of, 118

National Agricultural Library Thesaurus (NALT), 119–20

National Archives and Records Administration, 102

National Center for Atmospheric Research (NCAR), 106

National Center for Biotechnology Information (NCBI), 46, 55

National Center for Supercomputing Applications (NCSA), 100–102

National Centre for Text Mining (in UK), 67–68

National Coordination Office for Networking and Information Technology Research and Development (NCO/NIT), 79

National Digital Information Infrastructure and Preservation Program (NDIIPP), 107

National Digital Library for Agriculture (NDLA), 115, 122–24, 129

National Ecological Observatory Network (NEON), 101

National Endowment for the Humanities, 21, 85, 87

National Grid Service (in UK), 67

National Institutes of Health (NIH), 21, 53, 55, 57, 102

National Invasive Species Information Center (NISIC), 121

National Laboratory for Applied Network Research (NLANR), 101

National Lamda Rail, 71
National Library of Medicine (NLM), 21, 51, 54–55, 71, 115
National Science Board, 5, 34–35, 106
National Science Digital Library (NSDL), 105
National Science Foundation (NSF), 36, 73, 85, 95; agendas and priorities, 26, 33, 71; conferences, workshops, and reports, 25, 63–65, 67, 78, 96; leadership in E-science, 19–20; programs, 28, 82, 100–101; support for DataNet, 52, 57, 108; UCSD proposals submitted to, 106–8
National Technical Information Service (NTIS), 118
National Virtual Observatory (NVO), 5, 46, 93 n, 94–97
NCAR. See National Center for Atmospheric Research
NCBI. See National Center for Biotechnology Information
NCN. See Network for Computational Nanotechnology
NCO/NIT. See National Coordination Office for Networking and Information Technology Research and Development
NCSA. See National Center for Supercomputing Applications
NDIIPP. See National Digital Information Infrastructure and Preservation Program
NDLA. See National Digital Library for Agriculture
NEES. See Network for Earthquake Engineering Simulation
NEON. See National Ecological Observatory Network
Net@EDU program (of EDUCAUSE), 71
Network for Computational Nanotechnology (NCN), 39–40
Network for Earthquake Engineering Simulation (NEES), 101
Next Generation SDSC, 109
NIH. See National Institutes of Health
NISIC. See National Invasive Species Information Center

NLANR. See National Laboratory for Applied Network Research
NLM. See National Library of Medicine
Norman, Mike, 99 n
NSDL. See National Science Digital Library
NSF. See National Science Foundation
NTIS. See National Technical Information Service
Nutrition.gov, NAL Web site, 121–22
NVO. See National Virtual Observatory

OAI-ORE. See Open Archives Initiative Object Reuse and Exchange
Ocean Observatories Initiative (OOI), 101
Ocean Research Interactive Observatory Networks (ORION), 101
Office of Cyberinfrastructure, NSF, 36, 65, 73, 82
Office of Science and Innovation e-Infrastructure Working Group (in UK), 65
Office of Science and Technology (in UK), 19
OncoSpace Project, 95
Online Public Access Catalog, 119
ONSA program for human gene discovery, 80
OOI. See Ocean Observatories Initiative
Open access, 6, 54–55, 57
Open Archives Initiative, 18, 117
Open Archives Initiative Object Reuse and Exchange (OAI-ORE), 97
Open source movement, 13
Optical Society of America (OSA), 97
ORION. See Ocean Research Interactive Observatory Networks
OSA. See Optical Society of America

PACI. See Partnerships for Advanced Computational Infrastructure
Partnerships for Advanced Computational Infrastructure (PACI), 100–102
PDB. See Protein Data Bank
Peer-to-peer networks, 13
Pew Internet and American Life Project, 77, 89 n.1

PiiMS. *See* Purdue Ionomics Information Management System

Plant genetics, 38–39

Plant Genome Research Program (PLANTS), 101

PLANTS. *See* Plant Genome Research Program

PREMIS, 105

Preservation, 25, 68, 72, 83–84, 86; at NDLA, 126–27; at UCSD, 106–8. *See also* Chronopolis digital preservation program; DataNet; Data Trust Alliance; DigArch (Digital Archiving); NDIIPP; Web-At-Risk

Protein Data Bank (PDB), 78, 101

Proteomics, 123

Proteomics/genomics, 55

Publications, 8, 18–19, 26–27, 36, 41, 96; of USDA, 116, 118–19

PubMed, 48

Purdue Ionomics Information Management System (PiiMS), 39

Purdue University, 38–39, 51

Ranganathan, Shiyali Ramamrita, 36

Real-time Observatories, Applications, and Data Management Network (ROAD-Net), 101

Registries, 10–11

"Reinventing Science Librarianship" forum, 71

Relais system, 119

Repositories. *See* Data repositories

Research Councils in the UK, 55, 65–67

Research Data Strategy Working Group (in Canada), 70

Research Information Network (RIN) in UK, 65, 67

Revolutionizing Science and Engineering through Cyberinfrastructure (NSF), report, 19

RIN. *See* Research Information Network

ROADNet. *See* Real-time Observatories, Applications, and Data Management Network

Rural Information Center, 121

Salt, David, 38–39

San Diego Supercomputer Center: future of, 108–9; history of, 100–106; mission and focus of, 105; and UCSD Libraries, 105–6

Sarbanes-Oxley Act, 86

Scholarly communication, 8, 26–28, 36, 77

Science, changes in, 7

Science Commons, 27

Science Environment for Ecological Knowledge (SEEK), 101

Science libraries, roles and future, 51–52, 54. *See also* Libraries

Science magazine, 5

Scripps Institution of Oceanography, 105

SEEK. *See* Science Environment for Ecological Knowledge

Shaw, Ralph R., 119

Sheridan Libraries, Johns Hopkins University, 12, 96, 97

Shipsey, Ian, 38

Skills needed by librarians and "informationists," 6

Sky Server Web site, 94–95, 97

SLAC. *See* Stanford Linear Accelerator

Sloan Digital Sky Survey (SDSS), 93–97

Smarr, Larry, 100, 102

Social computing, 19

Society of American Archivists, 37

Special Libraries Association, 121

SRB middleware, 105

Standards, 7, 66, 102

Stanford Linear Accelerator (SLAC), 80

State of São Paulo Research Foundation in Brazil (FAPESP), 80

Storage Resource Broker, 101

Supercomputer Center Program (of NSF), 100

SuperJANET 5 high-speed network, 5, 67

Sustainable Digital Data Preservation and Access Network (DataNet), 50, 52–53, 57, 83, 108

Synthetic biology, 123, 127–28

Szalay, Alexander, 93 n, 94

TAIR. *See* Arabidopsis Information Resource, The

Taylor, John, 4, 19

Technology, phases of, 21

Technology Directions Committee (at UCSD), 102–3

Technology transfer, at Johns Hopkins University, 95; information center in NAL, 12

Teragrid, 93 n

Thorin, Suzanne, 22

Tools needed for E-science, 5–6, 46, 102–3, 125

To Stand the Test of Time: Long-term Stewardship of Digital Data Sets in Science and Engineering (Association of Research Libraries), report, 25, 35

Towards 2020 Science (Microsoft), report, 24, 54

Trefethen, A. E., 6

Trends in E-science, 18–19

Tufts University, 86

Turbulence Database Cluster at Johns Hopkins University, 95

2020 Science Group, 11

United Nations Information System, 118

University of California at Los Angeles, 85

University of California at San Diego, support for E-science, 51, 99–110

University of California Grid, 109

University of Chicago, 97

University of Edinburgh, 96

University of Illinois, Graduate School of Library and Information Science, 29, 100

University of Liverpool Library, Special Collections and Archives, 68

University of Manchester, School of Computer Science, 68

University of Maryland, 106–7

University of Minnesota Libraries, 49, 51

University of New Mexico, 12

University of North Carolina at Chapel Hill, 85

University of Pennsylvania Library, 49

University of Southampton, 68

University of Washington libraries, 48, 50, 54, 96

Users of digital information technology: studies of needs and behaviors, 46, 48–49, 51–52, 83, 109; trends in use, 125–26

Vassar College, 79

Virtual laboratories and organizations, 4, 8, 20, 27–28

Virtual research environments (VRE), 66, 68

VIVO architecture (at Cornell), 50

VOSpace environment, 97

Voyager integrated library system (of NAL), 119

VRE. *See* Virtual research environments

Water Quality Information Center, 121

Web, adaptive, 12–13

Web-At-Risk (collection at CDL), 108

Web Lab (at Cornell), 46

Web of Science, 48

Web 2.0, 11, 19, 82

Wikipedia, 99–100

Work flows, challenges of in science, 24

World Wide Web, 18, 21

About the
Editors and Contributors

G. SAYEED CHOUDHURY is associate dean of University Libraries at Johns Hopkins University, lecturer in its Department of Computer Science, and Hodson director of the Digital Research and Curation Center at Hopkins. He is also senior presidential fellow with the Council on Library and Information Resources.

AMY FRIEDLANDER is director of programs for the Council on Library and Information Resources. Previously, she was founding editor of *D-Lib Magazine*, published five monographs on large-scale infrastructure systems, and provided technical support for the National Digital Information Infrastructure and Preservation Program.

GERALD GEORGE, a writer, editor, and administrator, has been special projects associate of the Council on Library and Information Resources, communications director of the U.S. National Archives and Records Administration, and director of the National Historical Publications and Records Commission, in Washington, D.C.

JOAN K. LIPPINCOTT is associate executive director of the Coalition for Networked Information, in Washington, D.C. She has also served as research associate for the American Council on Education and has held library positions at Cornell University, George Washington University, Georgetown University, and SUNY Brockport.

WENDY PRADT LOUGEE is university librarian and McKnight presidential professor at the University of Minnesota—Twin Cities. Previously, she served as associate director for digital library services at the University of Michigan, Ann Arbor. She also has held library positions at Brown University and Wheaton College (Massachusetts).

RICHARD E. LUCE is vice provost and director of libraries at Emory University. Previously, he served as research library director at the Los Alamos National Laboratory, where he also was the leader of the Library Without Walls project. Earlier he held administrative positions in library network organizations in Florida and Colorado.

DEANNA B. MARCUM, chair of the Planning Committee for the Kanazawa library roundtables, is associate librarian of Congress for library services. Previously, she has been president of the Council on Library and Information Resources and dean of the School of Library and Information Science at The Catholic University of America.

JAMES L. MULLINS is dean of libraries and professor of library science at Purdue University. Previously, he held senior administrative positions in libraries at the Massachusetts Institute of Technology, Villanova, and Indiana University, where he was also a part-time professor in the School of Library and Information Science.

NEIL RAMBO is acting director of health sciences libraries and acting associate dean of university libraries at the University of Washington. Previously, he has been director of cyberinfrastructure initiatives and special assistant to the dean of university libraries for biosciences and E-science at the University of Washington.

BRIAN E. C. SCHOTTLAENDER is the Audrey Geisel university librarian at the University of California, San Diego. Previously, he held positions in the libraries of UCLA, the University of Arizona, and Indiana University. He has also been senior associate to the university librarian of the California Digital Library.

PETER R. YOUNG is chief of the Asian Division of the Library of Congress. He has also been director of the National Agricultural Library, executive director of the U.S. National Commission on Libraries and Information Science, and chief of the Cataloging Distribution Service at the Library of Congress.